BUT WE WERE BORN FREE

But We Were Born Free

by ELMER DAVIS

GREENWOOD PRESS, PUBLISHERS
WESTPORT, CONNECTICUT

To the Memory of
ERNST REUTER
A fighter for freedom
whom nobody ever scared.

AUTHOR'S NOTE

MOST of the material in this book was spoken before it was printed, as may perhaps be inferred from the style. In the winter and spring of 1953 I was going around the country, preaching sermons on the need of defending the freedom of the mind. The substance of most of these, following the general lines of the talk at Vassar but including much additional material (which has been brought up to date), makes up the first of these chapters.

The second, on a somewhat different but cognate subject, is taken from a speech at Yale partially reprinted in the *Progressive*, with the inclusion of material from the Stafford Little Lecture at Princeton and the Embree Lectures at Transylvania.

"News and the Whole Truth" was originally a discourse delivered to the University of Minnesota School of Journalism and the Twin Cities Press Club, with its substance repeated in altered form to the Boston Press Club and eventually published in the *Atlantic*.

"History in Doublethink" (from the *Saturday Review*) was not a lecture—merely an annoyed reaction to the smug self-assurance of certain people who think that because they were completely wrong twenty years ago they must be completely right now that they entertain diametrically opposite opinions. It has apparently not occurred to them that they could be wrong both times.

"Grandeurs and Miseries of Old Age" (from *Harper's*) was also an annoyed reaction—this time to a well-intended, but in my opinion fallacious, endeavor to persuade people who are getting older that all is for the best in the best of all possible worlds. I wish it were. This may seem to have no connection with the theme of the book; but you will find that it has.

"Are We Worth Saving?" was the 1953 Phi Beta Kappa oration at Harvard, later printed in *Harper's*, as well as in the *Harvard Alumni Bulletin*, and somewhat motivated by annoyance with the doctrines of Dr. Toynbee.

To all those who originally sponsored these speeches, or published their content, I am indebted for permission to republish.

It might seem from the foregoing that I live in a state of permanent annoyance. Not at all; there is plenty nowadays that is annoying, God knows; but there are also plenty of good people in the world. An unforeseen dividend of my missionary journeys was that I made the acquaintance of so many of the best of them—agreeable persons who were also good citizens, as unhappily is not always the case. I am afraid, however, that I was preaching mostly to just men and women who need no repentance.

ELMER DAVIS

Washington, November 1953

CONTENTS

BUT WE WERE BORN FREE

I

Through the Perilous Night

1.

MORE than eighteen hundred years ago a great historian wrote that "rare is the felicity of the times when you can think what you like and say what you think." That felicity has indeed been rare throughout human history. Tacitus himself had lived through times when it was suicidal to say what you thought, and hazardous to let it be suspected that you were thinking at all; he survived into a more tolerant age, but that lasted for only a few generations till the lid closed down again. Since then the lid has been on and off—mostly on. In the false dawn of the eighteenth century it was lifted once more; and the men who made our government thought they could guarantee that the lid would stay off by almost immediately writing into the Constitution as its very first amendment the guarantee of freedom of religion, of speech, of the press—all corollaries of the basic right to think what you like. That seemed to have settled that; with a great price our ancestors obtained this freedom, but we were born free.

So we were; but that freedom can be retained only by the eternal vigilance which has always been its price. In 1943 the Supreme Court declared that "if there is any fixed star in our constitutional constellation, it is that no official, high or petty, can prescribe what shall be orthodox in politics, nationalism, religion, or other matters of opinion; or force citizens to confess by word or act their faith therein." Since then, however, that fixed star has become somewhat obscured by clouds; and in 1953 the Ford Foundation found it advisable to allocate $15,000,000 to one of its subsidiaries, whose function was frankly stated as the restoring of respectability to the individual freedoms guaranteed by the Constitution.

Since the most conspicuous of recent encroachments on these freedoms had been the work of Congressional committees, Congress might have been expected to respond to this gesture; and it did. The Honorable Brazilla Carroll Reece of East Tennessee proposed, and the House of Representatives adopted (though not without a fight), a resolution to appoint a committee to investigate the tax-exempt foundations to see if they are using their money for un-American or subversive purposes. They had already been investigated

16

on that point a few months earlier, and all the big ones had been acquitted; but in Congressional jurisprudence no man (or institution) is ever acquitted. If a committee is weak enough to find him not guilty, you merely get another committee to try him again.

And while Mr. Reece, in his speech proposing the resolution, attacked all the big foundations, it was evidently the Ford Foundation that chiefly aroused his ire. Its endeavor to remove restrictions on freedom of thought, inquiry and expression was in his opinion subversion of our institutions (so now the Constitution itself is subversive); he said it would aid the Communist conspiracy, that the leaders of the Ford Foundation have a conception of civil liberty similar to that of the Communists—a comment he might more pertinently have applied to himself. But in spite of the observation of two Republican members, Mr. Fulton and Mr. Javits, that the resolution seemed aimed not at Communists but at people whose political and economic opinions differed from those of Mr. Reece, the House voted him his committee.

By coincidence, a Congressional committee that same day approved a bill to erect a monument to the freedoms guaranteed by the Constitution—the very freedoms that the Ford Foundation is trying to defend. The monument was to be erected right outside Arlington Cemetery. If Mr. Reece and those like him

17

have their way, it had better be put up inside the cemetery, along with the monuments to all the other distinguished dead.

This is of course only one incident in the attack now going on against these freedoms—an attack on various levels, federal, state and municipal, with the co-operation of many unofficial but zealous vigilantes—which, while it is nothing novel in our history, is worse than any other such crusade in my recollection. How far it is organized I do not know. Some people think they see evidence of what Senator McCarthy would call a pattern—a nation-wide conspiracy; I cannot discern it, though many of the crusaders certainly co-operate locally. (As they conspicuously do in Los Angeles, and as they did in Washington in the attack on Assistant Secretary of Defense Anna Rosenberg in December 1950; but respectable conservatives rallied to her support, and that venture soon proved to be a sinking ship; the rats jumped overboard, biting one another as they went.) But even if it is not nationally organized it is nationally dangerous; just as in a great air raid a hundred local fires may coalesce into a fire storm, in which the whole is greater than the sum of its parts, so local movements around the country add up into what seems to be a general attack not only on schools and colleges and libraries, on teachers and textbooks, but on all people who think and write (except reactionaries), an attack on freedom of inquiry, freedom of teaching, freedom of dissent—in short, on the freedom of the mind, the basic freedom from which all other freedoms spring.

Who is doing all this? Well, various kinds of people; it is hard to include them under one name. Reactionaries? But there are men who are reactionary in political and economic opinions and still do not approve of the suppression of thought. Fascists? But there are not very many real Fascists in this country; there are some—particularly conspicuous in the attacks on the schools and colleges—but it is hard to tell how many of them are Fascists on principle and how many are Fascists for revenue only, as the easiest way to shake down the rich for support of their committees and their magazines. They are no great danger anyway, for there is no longer a formidable and hostile foreign power, as there was fifteen years ago, to which they can give their allegiance; Peron's Argentina and Franco's Spain are hardly big enough to count. (Franco may prove, like Stalin, to be more dangerous when he is our ally than when we were barely on speaking terms with him.)

But if real Fascists are few, there is a dangerously large number of people—many but by no means all of them rich—who could be called Fascistoid. Fascism has to have at least a pretense of doctrine; in Italy the doctrine was ignored, in Germany it was never more than a thing of shreds and patches; but there is one cardinal principle that was not ignored in either country and seems to be sympathetically regarded by many people here—the principle that our side has a right to put your side down and keep you down, regardless. And a good deal of this has deeper motives than the mere joy of knocking people down and then kicking them. Gifford Phillips in an editorial in *Frontier* adds up some of the people who are doing this:

In league with the McCarthyists are the isolationists who hate the British and French and think we should withdraw from the UN; politically ignorant economic conservatives who see no difference between Socialism and Communism; the Machiavellians who pretend not to see any difference; the Asia-First, China Lobby crowd; the antifeminists; the extreme economic conservatives. . . . McCarthyism is a most useful device for this coalition because it can be (and has been) used successfully to undermine public confidence in those groups that oppose its program—labor groups, minority groups, ministerial groups, Fair Dealers and liberal Democrats, liberal Republicans (the attack on them is cautious right now), liberal journalists, writers, educators and other professional people.

Mr. Phillips has cited most of the participants in the antifreedom crusade, but not all. The elements he

20

mentions might be called (God help us) an elite; they have a good deal of influence, a great deal of money, and even some ideas, twisted and erroneous as those ideas may be. But they are backed up by a popular support—people who have little money, no influence except as they derive it from numbers, and nothing that could be called ideas; but plenty of emotion. The kind of people who a generation ago made up the mass membership of the Ku Klux Klan, which a few smart men at the top manipulated in their own interest; and I am afraid there are more of them now than there were then. I have guessed that people like that may amount to fifteen or twenty per cent of the population of the country, and hope that estimate is not too low—as some of my friends think whose material for a guess is as good as mine. People, they are, whose dominant surface emotion is hatred; but underlying that, besides an appalling ignorance, is fear. They are afraid to think because it is hard work, afraid to let other people think because it might turn out that what they themselves have always thought is wrong. It hurts more to have a belief pulled than to have a tooth pulled, and no intellectual novocain is available.

In so far as their fear has any logical basis, it implies that the principles of freedom on which this republic was founded will not stand examination. I ran into an instance of that a few years ago, on an official if not an intellectual level where you would hardly expect it. A girl who had been a Wave during the war wanted to get back into the Navy as a civilian employee; she gave me as a reference, and a security officer of Naval Intelligence came around to check up on her. I gave her a glowing recommendation, as I conscientiously could; I spoke highly not only of her loyalty but of her intelligence—— At which he frowned. "These intelligent people," he said, "are very likely to be attracted to Communism."

This opinion is far from unique. Our present procedures for checking the loyalty of government employees, or applicants for employment, seem well calculated to insure that there will be no excess of intelligence or independence of thinking in the public service hereafter. A good many thousand government workers, who have already undergone two loyalty or security investigations and have been cleared, must now go through the wringer a third time, now that the standards have been stiffened.

But while the standards have been stiffened, definitions have been changed, in a kindlier sense. Any government must get rid not only of employees of doubtful loyalty but of security risks—people in sensitive positions, with access to secret information, who talk and/or drink too much, or whose behavior lays them open to blackmail. The Truman loyalty program discriminated between these classes; people were fired either on loyalty or security grounds, and it was generally known on which. The Eisenhower administration charitably swept the two groups together, on the general standard that employment of the individual must be found consistent with national security. It was explained, and was no doubt intended, that this would remove the stigma of dismissal for disloyalty: it could always be supposed that anybody who was fired was a mere security risk.

This theory betrayed little knowledge of human nature as it has been educated in recent years; if the boundary between security and disloyalty is wiped out, they must all be disloyal. In the first few months of operation 1,456 people were fired—the majority of them as security risks. But the President's own lawyer, telling the Advertising Club of New Jersey about "the Middle Way of the Eisenhower Administration," boasted that "1,456 subversives have been kicked out of government jobs"; and the headline, even in the New York *Times*, naturally translated this into "1,456 Reds."

Yet the majority of them were only security risks— a term liberally interpreted. People like that are sitting ducks for the sleuthhounds of security; real Communists, members of the surviving hard core of the party, if any of them are still in the government service, are probably too smart to be caught. As Norman

23

Thomas says, if you burn down the barn to get rid of the rats, the rats usually escape; it is the horses that perish.

Fear of intelligence, fear of thinking, fear to trust your own opinions in the give and take of discussion—this in the strongest nation in the world, a nation which only a decade ago put forth the greatest military effort in all history (nothing the Germans or the Russians ever did equaled the simultaneous achievements of Eisenhower's invasion of Normandy and Spruance's conquest of the Marianas), a nation that could do the same again if it had to—provided we had the guts, provided we had not let our bowels turn to water. How many of our fellow citizens have become afraid of their own shadows I do not know; but there are far too many—"morticians of the mind," ex-President Truman has called them—and there are plenty of ambitious politicians who find, in making them afraid of their own shadows, the road to power. Above all McCarthy.

I regret that I have to mention McCarthy; I regret that he exists. But he does exist, and not to mention him would be as if people in a malarial country refused to mention the anopheles mosquito. (There is a quinine that can neutralize his venom; it is called courage. It does not seem to be widely distributed in the upper ranks of our government.) This cam-

24

paign would exist if McCarthy did not exist, but it would be much less effective; his extraordinary and too long underestimated talents as a rabble rouser have earned him his position as Master of the Revels. There is a theory that McCarthy was made by the newspapers, which is true only in a limited degree. He has a remarkable gift for turning up with stories that would be important if true, and a still more remarkable agility in evasive action; as fast as one of his phonies is exposed he hits the front page with another which won't be exposed till tomorrow; and how many people read the second-day story? The newspapers could not have ignored his early attacks on the State Department and the violent Senate debate they provoked; the Senators could not have ignored them either. It does seem that now that it has been amply demonstrated that nothing McCarthy says can be accepted as true without corroboration the newspapers might be more careful in the way they deal with his "exposures." One or two newspapers have worked out methods for handling the news about him that might keep the reader from being misled; but this practice has not spread widely, for it conflicts with the doctrine of the American news industry that if a Senator says it, it is news, whether there is any truth in it or not.

And certainly there is nothing in the belief held

25

by many well-meaning citizens that if people would only stop talking about McCarthy he would evaporate. That might have been true in his early days; but now he is chairman of a powerful Senate committee, legally entitled to investigate government operations (and branching out into the investigation of other matters that are none of his business); he maintains a personal spy system, financed from sources largely undisclosed, to get something which can be used (usually in distorted form) against American officials at home or abroad; and he has created a situation in which the reputation and the livelihood of any public official is pretty much at the mercy of a jealous or incompetent co-worker, a discharged servant, a divorced wife or an ex-mistress. I do not think he is a Fascist; I do not even think he is a Communist, though a Communist assigned to undermine the government of the United States at home and make it ridiculous abroad would do just about what he is doing; he is a McCarthyist, and a very successful one. He has already cashed in heavily on fear, and even if people quit talking about him he would go on working.

But, they tell us, there is something to be afraid of—something terrible—Communism. Well, Communism is dangerous, but they are not afraid of it where it exists, where it is powerful and dangerous, in Rus-

26

sia; these antifreedom crusaders show no interest in Russia at all. They are unable to distinguish, as Philip Rahv once wrote, between Communism as a danger *to* America and Communism as a danger *in* America; or, as George Kennan put it, they think Communism is something invented in this country about 1945. (This view, once confined to the unlettered, seems to be spreading into the more influential circles. There are some just-below-the-top-level members of the administration who, if asked to name the two most important and dangerous Communists of recent years, would give you not Stalin and Malenkov, but Alger Hiss and Harry Dexter White.) I have no doubt that many of the crusaders—especially the unofficial vigilantes—really believe that Communism is a purely American phenomenon, but they have a strange conception of Communism. It is merely opinions different from their own. Some of the most active crusaders, however, are not after Communism at all. It is hard to know what to call the people they really are attacking, since "liberals" and "progressives" are both terms that have been discredited by some of the people who have used them; but we know what they used to mean, and they describe the targets of this crusade. They are after people who think for themselves and whose thinking does not agree with theirs— in so far as what they do can be called thinking.

27

McCarthy has made this evident enough. In the winter of 1953, when there promised to be great competition between Congressional committees for the privilege of investigating Communists in the schools (finally settled by letting two of them do it at once while the third went on to even juicier fields), McCarthy, shrewder than his competitors, said he was going after not merely Communists but Communist thinkers. The distinction was prudent: whether a man is a Communist is a matter of fact, though the fact may sometimes be hard to determine; but a Communist thinker is anybody whose thinking you choose to regard as Communist. McCarthy presently gave us his definition; his examination of Jim Wechsler made it clear that in his opinion a Communist is anybody who criticizes McCarthy. He had already called the Milwaukee *Journal* and the Washington *Post* local editions of the *Daily Worker;* some sense of prudence has up to this time prevented him from calling the weekly *America,* which has also criticized him, the Jesuit edition of the *Daily Worker;* but give him time. Indeed his line of thinking had become apparent during the Presidential campaign, with his attack on the "Communist" influences around Stevenson. In his usual manner, when he is not protected by the immunity of the Senate floor, he didn't quite call these men Communists, but the innuendo was clear. Wil-

28

son Wyatt, Arthur Schlesinger, Jr., Jim Wechsler, Archie MacLeish, "Richard" De Voto—men who were fighting Communism long before McCarthy ever discovered it as a paying issue; when he was beating Bob La Follette out of the senatorial nomination with the aid of Communist votes, and later when he was using propaganda from German Communists to save the lives of Nazi officers who had murdered American prisoners at Malmédy.

So a Communist is anybody you don't agree with. (Even Robert Alphonso Taft was once called a follower of the Communist line by a real-estate lobbyist because he was in favor of public housing.) And a good many of our citizens, in the name of anti-Communism, would suppress the freedoms guaranteed by the Constitution which are one of the principal differences between a free and a totalitarian society.

It has been argued that the Founding Fathers could not foresee the international Communist conspiracy; if they had, they would never have adopted the Bill of Rights. This has a certain superficial plausibility; only a few years after our government got started it was faced with a comparable movement—Jacobinism, which, starting as a world-wide crusade for liberty, soon became an agency of French imperialism. Accordingly, some of the Founding Fathers—by no means all—supported the Sedition Act of 1798, which

29

made it a crime to write or say anything false, scandalous or malicious against the President or Congress with intent to bring them into disrepute. (As Federalist judges interpreted it the word "false" was apt to be ignored.) Then as now the pretext was fear that some of our citizens were loyal to a dangerous foreign power rather than to their own country; then as now, many honest but thickheaded citizens were convinced that any disagreement with their own opinions was disloyalty; then as now, this sentiment was skillfully used by reactionary politicians to try to ruin men and suppress opinions that they didn't like, even though there was no taint of disloyalty about them.

That, however, was a very different matter from the present attack on freedom; it was a duly enacted law, designed to keep in power an administration and a party which had lost the confidence of the people; and being a law, it could be repealed. It was repealed, though too late to save the Federalist party. The men who enacted it had forgotten that there was a practical as well as a philosophical justification for the Bill of Rights, at least in a country which still had free elections, so that the government could change hands; legalized repression could be exercised by whichever party was in power, and the logical end of that would have been such proscriptions and counterproscriptions as distinguished the last days of the Roman Republic.

If false, scandalous and malicious attacks on the President and Congress had still been a crime in the first fifteen years of the nineteenth century, a good many eminent Federalists would have gone to jail— some of them with good reason, for they were actually meditating and plotting treason. But Jefferson believed and said that error of opinion may be tolerated so long as truth is free to combat it; and on that principle (with occasional lapses) we have operated ever since. We are still operating on it, in theory; recent statutory restrictions on the freedom of speech have not been very serious; but there has been terrific extralegal pressure from those who feel that truth cannot be tolerated, even when error is free to combat it. Men do not now go to jail, unless they are imprudent enough to perjure themselves before Congressional committees; they merely lose their jobs and their reputations—sometimes with reason but more often not; for the procedures of some Congressional committees I have seen in action—notably the Internal Security Committee under Senator McCarran's chairmanship—would have shocked even such a Federalist fanatic as Mr. Justice Samuel Chase.

All this has created what has correctly been called a climate of fear; to call it a reign of terror is certainly a very considerable exaggeration on a national

31

basis, though locally a good many people have been terrorized. This exaggeration has been particularly prevalent abroad; some of it, particularly in a small section of the English press, is due if not to malice at least to *Schadenfreude*. But there is some excuse for it among foreigners whose knowledge of the United States is limited, particularly if they happen to have seen what could be called a reign of terror among American officials in Germany, created by the performances of Cohn and Schine. As Joseph C. Harsch reported to the *Christian Science Monitor:*

> A European looks around him and sees actual evidence of an American police power operating in Europe which owes its allegiance not to the American government but to Senator McCarthy. He has personal agents in many European countries. They interview Europeans about American government officials. They interview servants, and European government officials. There is in fact a private secret police force working for Senator McCarthy; and to any and every European a private police force means just one thing, an instrument of power outside the existing and regular government. This condition has always, in European experience, led to an extra-constitutional seizure of power.

No wonder the Europeans are worried; no wonder Americans who see that sort of thing at first hand are worried too.

32

Reactionary writers who approve the results of this crusade, though they are a little too respectable to take part in it themselves, are fond of saying, "Who's getting hurt? Whose freedom is restricted?" People say to me, "You can still talk, can't you, and nobody stops you?" No, nobody has stopped me yet, because my employers are men of courage; about once a week somebody tries it. As to who's getting hurt, plenty of schoolteachers, college professors, and librarians could give you the answer. The National Educational Association reported recently, after studying five hundred school systems, that there is less academic freedom in the country than there was in 1940; that teachers are reluctant to discuss controversial subjects for fear of local reprisals.

Arthur Sulzberger, publisher of the New York *Times,* said not long ago that there has been dropped upon utterance and ideas a smoke screen of intimidation that dims essential thought and essential speech; if the publisher of the best and perhaps the strongest newspaper in the country feels that way, how much more must lesser men feel it? The *Times,* conspicuously, has not been intimidated, though I have no doubt it has been tried; neither have the publications that McCarthy has directly attacked—the Milwaukee *Journal,* the Washington *Post,* the New York *Post, Time* magazine. Nor have other newspapers—nota-

33

bly the Denver *Post* and the St. Louis *Post-Dispatch*. But a good many editors seem to feel that if you pretend you don't see it, it isn't there.

This was made evident by the fiasco of the action of the Society of Newspaper Editors when Jim Wechsler of the New York *Post* asked them if McCarthy's attack on him was not an infringement on the freedom of the press. A committee of eleven men was appointed—its chairman, Russ Wiggins of the Washington *Post*. It deliberated solemnly and finally came to the conclusion—at least seven of its eleven members did—that if it were an infringement on the freedom of the press that would be a bad thing, but they couldn't decide whether it was or not. Ask one of these seven for whom the bell tolls, and he won't know till it is ringing right beside his desk.

Four others—Chairman Wiggins, Herbert Brucker, William Tugman and Eugene Pulliam, Jr.—said it *was* an attack on the freedom of the press and they didn't like it; whereupon McCarthy demanded that the Society of Newspaper Editors investigate Wiggins and his paper. The editors, displaying a courage with which few would have credited them, ignored this demand. But meanwhile a number of highly reputable journalists had argued that, since McCarthy's attack had in fact failed to intimidate Wechsler, it was no attack on the freedom of the press at all. This amounts to saying that attempted rape is no crime if the girl is lucky enough to fight off her assailant.

Newspapermen are supposed to be better able than most people to see and to understand what is happening. For the mass supporters of this obscurantist crusade an excuse is offered—that the international situation is on their nerves; it causes apprehension, and the fact that the average citizen can do nothing about it creates frustration. The excuse would be more impressive if these people showed any interest in the Russian danger (even the reactionaries in Congress show little interest when it comes to appropriations for defense); but it is undeniably true that we live in a world of danger and tension, a tension which is likely to continue a good many years longer. We face a very powerful and dangerous foreign enemy— two enemies indeed, Russia and China—whose rulers are animated by a creed that makes truly peaceful coexistence impossible so long as they take that creed seriously; yet nobody in this country wants to solve that situation by war if it can prudently be avoided. So what should a mature and intelligent nation do in such a crisis? Why, we ought to keep our heads, keep our nerves steady, refuse to be upset by trivial provocations but be alert to really serious dangers; we ought to distinguish between our real friends and our

35

real enemies, make an accurate identification of the direction of the peril and a correct appreciation of its magnitude. In short, we ought to think—a right denied in totalitarian countries to anybody but a few men at the top, whose thinking is warped by dogma; but guaranteed to us by the Constitution. The right to think is the real difference between us and the enemy; it is likely to give us ultimate victory in the cold war—or in a hot war, if that should break out.

That is what a mature and intelligent nation ought to do and what many of our citizens are doing. But many others, unable to find a better outlet for their frustration, take it out on their less influential neighbors, in the mood of a man who, being afraid to stand up to his wife in a domestic argument, relieves his feelings by kicking the cat. (As anybody who knows me will tell you, I have the most profound detestation for people who kick cats.) It is people like that who make up much of the mass support for McCarthyism.

A few instances, out of many that might be cited. In Houston, a man and his wife—she a radio writer— were sitting in a Chinese restaurant talking to the proprietor about a radio program which they hoped he would sponsor—a program dealing with recent Chinese history. A man who overheard them rushed out and telephoned to the police that they were "talking Communist"; so they were promptly arrested. What they were said to have said—whether they did say it or not is not clear—was that Chiang Kai-shek was fighting a losing battle. That may or may not have been true—especially depending on whether it meant his hanging on in Formosa or reconquering the mainland; but true or false, it was no evidence of Communism. Yet this couple spent the night in jail—fourteen hours in jail—before the police finally concluded they had nothing on them and let them go.

One of my listeners sent me a full account of this affair, on the front page of the Houston *Press,* and I remarked that if the time ever came when that sort of thing was not on the front page, we would be in a bad way. Thereupon other listeners reported that another Houston paper had put it on page seven in section three, while the third hadn't found it worthy of mention at all. Now these do not seem to have been important people. If some prominent citizen of Houston—say Jesse Jones, not to mention the oil zillionaires who have lately zoomed past him—had had to spend the night in jail, it would have been on every front page. Of course this would never have happened to Jesse Jones; the police would only have had to find out who he was to let him go (no doubt on the theory that he could never say anything unorthodox). But if there is one law for Jesse Jones and another for ordinary people, the time could come when there is no law except the whim of the police, even for Jesse Jones.

The American Legion post in Lincoln, Nebraska, had been having some membership troubles; so the Legion's state director of Americanism came to talk to them and suggested that if they could find some good Communist literature and really fight it they could get more members. He remarked that a certain professor at the state university was using a certain textbook which the students couldn't swallow; he didn't say the professor was a Communist, but the innuendo was clear. There had indeed been two or three phone calls to the Legion from students who objected to the book; two of them also objected that the professor was a Democrat. One of them said the book was presented as gospel truth which could not be contradicted, and this, if true, would have been a grave indictment of the professor; but many students came forward to declare that it was not true. The book—which had been selected by the professor on the basis of reviews in scholarly publications as the best he could get—was used as a basis for discussion and was freely criticized by students and the professor himself.

One gratifying consequence of this attack was that people stood up on their hind legs and roared in protest against it—the faculty, the student body, many

38

people in the town. The Legion soon showed signs of wanting to let go of the hot potato and presently passed it to the regents of the university, who, so far as I have heard up to this time, have done nothing about it.

But there was a still more interesting aspect to this episode—it was an example of the new theory of literary and artistic criticism. The book was published by one of the best commercial publishers, but under the auspices—whatever that means—of the Institute of Pacific Relations, which was then being kicked around by the McCarran committee; it was edited by Lawrence Rosinger, and one chapter was by Owen Lattimore. Now I have not read this book; disinterested persons who have read it could find nothing subversive in it. But apparently nobody in the Legion ever read it either. If they did, they did not find the fact worth mentioning, either in their original protest or in their letter to the regents some weeks later; nor did they offer any specific criticisms of its content. All they know is who wrote it. As they said, "The sponsorship of the Institute of Pacific Relations makes the book suspect. The contribution of Owen Lattimore makes the book suspect. The editorship of Lawrence Rosinger makes the book suspect."

Suspect—a historic word; the favorite word of Robespierre in the Reign of Terror when he was marking

39

off somebody for the guillotine. "He is suspect"; that was enough. And many people seem to hold that it is still enough, to damn not only a man but his works, no matter what is in them. In the winter of 1952-53 the American Legion all over the country was picketing the theaters showing Charlie Chaplin's latest picture. I have not seen this picture—not because I am afraid to go through picket lines but because I seldom have time to see pictures; but I read many reviews of it, none of which found anything subversive in it. So far as I know, the Legion never claimed there was anything subversive in it; all they know is who made it—a man whose associations and alleged political opinions they don't like; one of their leaders around Washington said that if you buy a ticket to a Chaplin picture you are trading with the enemy. Among the musical compositions that were to have been played in President Eisenhower's inaugural festivities was Aaron Copland's "Lincoln Portrait." On the protest of a Chicago congressman it was thrown out—not because it is not good music, not because it was an inadequate representation of Lincoln, but because the congressman disapproved of Copland's associations and alleged opinions.

Till that happened, I thought the United States was growing up. In 1917-18 Wagner's operas could not be played in this country because he was a German. In the late war there would have been far more reason for banning Wagner; he was one of the spiritual ancestors of Nazism; indeed the first Nazi ever portrayed on the stage was Siegfried. But in 1941 everybody decided that if it is good music the political opinions of the composer do not make it suspect, and we all went to see *The Ring* with as much enjoyment as ever. This sensible rule, applied to Fascist sympathizers, apparently does not apply—like some other rules—to people suspected of Communist sympathies. In the spring of 1953 the Veterans of Foreign Wars extracted a promise from the Voice of America that it would not put on its programs any of the music of Roy Harris, who in 1943 had composed a symphony which he dedicated to the Soviet Union. Maybe you remember 1943—a year when we were engaged in a great war in which the Russians (through no fault of their own) were our allies, a war whose outcome was then still undecided. The Russian victory at Stalingrad was one of the battles that decided it. At that time the most important thing in the world was to kill Germans, and the Russians were killing more of them than anybody else; there was reason for dedicating a symphony, in 1943, to the Soviet Union. Why Harris did not later withdraw his dedication (on demand) as Beethoven, without demand, had withdrawn his dedication of the "Eroica" to Napoleon, I do not know. I am not acquainted with Mr. Harris; maybe he still likes the Soviet Union, or maybe he just didn't like the demand. Maybe he doesn't like to be pushed around; and if this country ever runs out of people who don't like to be pushed around, we are done for.

This now seems to be the primary criterion of modern literary and artistic criticism: never mind what is in it—all you need to know is who did it; if he is suspect, it doesn't matter what is in it. It may seem surprising that people who feel that way have not picketed the numerous art galleries where Picasso's pictures are hung; but they probably never heard of Picasso.

2.

These extralegal pressures could be discouraged, though not stopped, if high officials spoke up against them; but officials who did so might alienate voters; the candidate who defended the freedom of the mind before the American Legion convention lost the election (probably not for that reason, but politicians hate to take chances); and up to this writing (November) the executive branch of the government has done little to defend even its own officials against the anti-freedom campaign. Meanwhile, Congressional committees—some of them—have been running wild; and I mean wild.

The work of Congressional investigating committees, if not essential to good government—some well-governed countries manage to get along without anything of the sort—can at least under our system be a great contribution to good government when the committees are decently conducted, as the majority of them are. But some of them have so behaved that even members of Congress have questioned what they are doing no less than the way they are doing it. The theory of Congressional investigation is that it is to provide information which might be the basis for action by Congress—that is, passing a law. But it is a serious question whether Congress has a right to investigate in fields where the Constitution forbids it to legislate, as some committees did last year.

Even where that constitutional uncertainty does not intrude, there may be doubt as to the pertinence, if not the authority, of the investigation. In September 1953 Senator McCarthy announced that his committee, or what was left of it after resignations, was going to investigate atrocities against American prisoners in Korea—something which the Army was already investigating—and also the detention of some prisoners in Manchuria after the armistice. (Really to investigate that, a man would have to go to Man-

43

churia, but McCarthy did not volunteer.) Anyway, Representative Kenneth B. Keating, Republican of upstate New York, whose own committee under his chairmanship had been a model of fairness in investigation, told the New York State Bar Association that he could not see much point in such an investigation since it "had no demonstrable relation to the lawmaking function." So far as he could see, said Mr. Keating, Congress could do nothing to remedy that situation; passing a law wouldn't get the prisoners out of Manchuria.

Mr. Keating went even further. He said he didn't think Congress "should invade areas where its only purpose is to assemble facts for the amusement or edification" of a public which seems avid for entertainment rather than for information about the workings of government. But he went on to say—with a truth that cannot be denied—that it seems to be more effective with the press gallery "to be sensational or contentious than to be fair, reasonable, or even to be right," and that it seems to pay big political dividends.

To be sure, a couple of days later Mr. Keating, following the example of greater men, explained that of course he wasn't talking about McCarthy; but he had certainly made a pointed summary of the case against Senator Joe Doakes and against some—not all—Congressional committees. They invade fields where Con-

44

gress could do nothing; they function substantially as package television shows for the entertainment of the public; they have (I am talking only about some committees, remember) little concern for accuracy and still less for the rights of the defendant (theoretically there are no defendants, only witnesses, but many of these hearings are substantially criminal trials); and the chief product of all this uproar is publicity—especially for the chairman of the committee—the publicity that leads to power. It is not so with many committees; it does not have to be so with any of them. Either House could, if it wished, adopt a code of fair procedure binding on all its committees; various members of both Houses (including Mr. Keating) have proposed such codes; but none of them has been adopted nor is ever likely to be until we elect fewer cowards to Congress, and fewer blatherskites who will do anything for publicity.

In the meantime, the behavior of a committee usually depends on the character of its chairman. The famous House Un-American Activities Committee, whose conduct under the chairmanship of J. Parnell Thomas was a national scandal, calmed down after he left his seat in Congress to go to jail. For the next four years, under the chairmanship of John S. Wood and the effective leadership of Francis Walter, its hearings were usually conducted with propriety and

45

fairness. Then, with the change of party control in January 1953, there succeeded to the chairmanship the bouncy Mr. Harold Velde of Illinois, who evidently decided to make things hum.

The same change of party control brought to the chairmanship of the Senate Internal Security Committee—whose field of operations would normally bring it into competition with the Un-American Activities Committee—Mr. Jenner of Indiana in place of Mr. McCarran, who had devoted most of his attention to the Institute of Pacific Relations. I shall have more to say later about the McCarran Committee, whose operations I frequently observed. Under its new chairman the Internal Security Committee is hardly what it used to be. In McCarran's day it was bipartisan but monolithic—seven souls with but a single thought, which bore a close resemblance to the thought of Mr. Alfred Kohlberg. Now four new members have been added, two of whom seem to have predilections toward fairness; also, the new chairman is not the man his predecessor was. Ethically there seems little to choose between them; but Jenner has nothing like the intellect and force of Old Silvertop. His chief claim to fame is the speech in which he said that General Marshall is a living lie, not only willing but eager to play the role of a front man for traitors—that, and his subsequent suggestion that the Korean

46

peace conference would go better if we didn't let the enemy attend it.

But the principal effect of the change in party control was that it brought McCarthy to the chairmanship of the Senate Government Operations Committee, of whose subcommittee on investigations he promptly made himself the head. Theretofore, he had been pretty much of a lone wolf, though a few of his colleagues occasionally ran in the pack with him; thereafter his inquisitions were backed by the authority of the United States Government.

American schools and colleges, already under many local attacks, were further threatened in the winter of 1953 when all three of these committees announced an intention to investigate them. They all promised to keep out of one another's way, but it was evident that they would have to go over pretty much the same material and the same people. The constitutional prohibition of double jeopardy couldn't stop them; that applies only to the courts. One committee after another can bring the same man before them and compel him to tell the same story over again—which offers the hopeful possibility that there may be discrepancies in his testimony so that you can indict him for perjury. Unless, of course, he happens to be one of the professional ex-Communist informers who seem to constitute a pool on which any Congressional com-

47

mittee can draw. In that case discrepancies in his testimony are disregarded.

Education had reason to tremble at the prospect of investigation by Jenner, Velde and McCarthy; all of them, in advance, were breathing out threatenings and slaughter, with McCarthy gleefully predicting that there would be "an awful lot of screaming about academic freedom." Beyond that, what were the qualifications of the investigators? Jenner's I have discussed; Velde was chiefly known, before he came to his chairmanship, for the introduction of a bill in the previous session—for a wonder, nothing was done about it—requiring the Librarian of Congress to go through the books in his library, all nine million of them, and mark any and all subversive passages. And suppose that Librarian Luther Evans, after completing this fairly extensive course of required reading, had failed to mark as subversive certain material that looked subversive to Velde—assuming that Velde had ever read it? Then, presumably, we should have to get a new Librarian. Conceivably, this might have been one of the reasons that led Luther Evans to resign his job and become head of UNESCO—a fairly hot spot itself, but farther away from Capitol Hill.

As for McCarthy—— Archbishop Richard J. Cushing of Boston—has said that "despite any extremes, or mistakes that might have been made, I don't believe anything has brought the evils and methods of Communism more to the attention of the American people than his investigations." This amounts to saying that nothing brings the danger of fire more to the attention of the public than turning in false alarms all over town. I cannot recall that all his "exposures," before he became a committee chairman, had ever got a single Communist; since then he seems to have caught a few minnows, but no big fish. No wonder. He was not after Communist fish; he was after people, including a few ex-Communists who are now active and effective anti-Communists, whose opinions disagree with his; and whom he has smeared by all sorts of distortions and misrepresentations. The Archbishop's praise of him would seem to imply that the end justifies the means. I do not at all suppose that that was intended, but if it had been it would still be wrong, for McCarthy has not attained his professed end, of bringing the evils and methods of Communism to the attention of the people, though he *has* attained what seems to have been his real end, of persuading many people that all liberals are Communists.

For his methods, a few examples out of hundreds will be enough. In his early investigation of the Voice of America he told two flat falsehoods about what had happened in secret session where no reporters were present to check up on him. He said that Mrs.

Roosevelt had tried to persuade the State Department to use the writings of Howard Fast in American propaganda overseas. She had not; she had tried to persuade them to reverse a decision, made under senatorial pressure, not to use the works of Harry Overstreet. McCarthy totally misrepresented the contents of a very intelligent propaganda directive, and scared the State Department into withdrawing it. A few days later, however, he seems to have discovered that some reporters knew what the directive really said— virtually the opposite of what he had first reported— so he came out with the true text, apparently confident that he had something else good for that day's headline so that few people would notice the contradiction. Since then there have been similar incidents.

And there was furthermore the matter of McCarthy's financial transactions, which he declined to explain to a Senate committee but which, the committee declared, raise an issue which goes to the very core of the Senate's authority, integrity and the respect in which it is held by the people. You might suppose that the Senate would look into an issue so important as that, but it did not; some senators regarded McCarthy as too valuable an asset to his party to be discredited; others, knowing his methods of retaliation, were simply scared.

The committee, to be sure, turned over this information to the Department of Justice. Attorney General McGranery was going out of office in two weeks when the report came in; he did nothing about it. Attorney General Brownell's department mulled over it for a long time and finally came up with the conclusion that the evidence showed no technical violations of law. This can hardly be called a glowing vindication of McCarthy; but a miss is as good as a mile.

These were the men who announced, in the winter of 1953, that they were going to investigate American education. What right they had to investigate it is open to some doubt; schools and state universities are under the jurisdiction of state authorities, and the authority of Congress over private institutions is not clear to me—in spite of a memorandum a year ago from the staff of the Internal Security Committee, quoted with approval by Senator Ferguson, which declared that it is the duty of Congress to see that educational institutions implant only sound ideas in the minds of students. This is not among the powers granted to Congress by the Constitution. The First Amendment says that Congress shall make no law abridging the freedom of speech; it does not say "except in schools and colleges." It also forbids abridgment of the freedom of the press, or the making of any law prohibiting the free exercise of religion. Yet

51

the colleges, the churches and the press all came under Congressional inquisition in the year 1953.

The excuse is that these freedoms were not being abridged, that Congress was only going after individual teachers, clergymen or editors who happened to be Communists. But the only editor attacked, most clergymen who were attacked, and some of the teachers, were not Communists. The colleges admitted the legitimacy of these investigations, but whether as a matter of law or of public relations is unknown to me; it was obvious that any one which refused to cooperate would be smeared as a nest of Communism. It is true that some of them recognized limits; as Dr. Conant said in his farewell report at Harvard, "the independence of each college and university would be threatened if governmental agencies of any sort started inquiries into the nature of the instruction that was given." But you can get the same effect, without specifically going into the nature of the instruction, by putting the heat on every teacher who gives a certain kind of instruction—as every reactionary school board knows, and every reactionary college trustee. Since, however, these are the legal controllers of the schools and colleges, this is perhaps not an interference with their independence, even if it plays hell with academic freedom and ultimately with the standing of the school or college.

Academic freedom. I have heard and read many arguments this past year on its definition, and even participated in one or two. I have heard it claimed by Communists on the witness stand; but if they are genuine blown-in-the-glass Communists (and I doubt if there are any others left in this country any more), the claim was phony. They have no such freedom; they must obey the orders of their party when it gives orders. There is certainly no academic freedom in Russia, where history is rewritten to suit the changing party line, as in Orwell's *1984;* and even geneticists must accept and teach the doctrines of Lysenko because the Central Committee of the Communist party says they are true.

We are a long way from that, even though some of our fellow citizens are trying to bring us around to it, even though I do not doubt that there are college teachers who find it advisable not to teach what the chairman of the board of trustees regards as untrue. Academic freedom, I should think, is the right of any man professionally qualified by study and experience to teach anything that honestly seems to him to be true, without reprisal. Sidney Hook, whose anti-Communism I do not suppose even McCarthy would question, holds that we should protect the academic freedom of any man who as a result of his own study and experiments concludes that the doctrines of Ly-

53

senko are true, though not if he accepts them because the Communist party tells him to. I should think that the professional qualifications of such a man might be regarded with some skepticism; but as Hook reminds us, so much that used to be scientific heresy is now regarded as scientific truth that we cannot afford to shut the door on any honest speculator.

This conception of academic freedom does not seem to be widely held in Congress. Nevertheless, not much of the damage that was anticipated from these investigations has occurred. It cannot be said that it was prevented by the effective defense of the educators, which was very spotty; some of them stood up, some caved in. It did not occur because McCarthy has not yet got around to education, finding government a more profitable field; because Jenner, whatever his other qualities, lacks the relentless vindictiveness of McCarran; and because Velde turned out to be so inept that the friends of freedom may reasonably regard him as their secret weapon.

Velde's quality was shown very early. Agnes Meyer (Mrs. Eugene Meyer, wife of the publisher of the Washington *Post*) had questioned his qualifications as an investigator of American education. Velde came right back at her—foolishly, in a talk with reporters, where he did not have his constitutional immunity on the floor of Congress—declaring that she was an intellectual pinko. For proof he offered a letter which he said she had written to the magazine *Soviet Russia Today* praising Russia—a letter quoted with approval by *Pravda*. It needed only a glance at the files of the magazine, and of *Pravda*, to show that the letter had been written not by Mrs. Eugene Meyer of the District of Columbia but by a Mrs. G. S. Mayer of British Columbia. Velde was told of that three hours later; he apologized thirty-six hours later, and fired the employee who had given him the information—a man whose record was such that he should never have been employed at all. But when the facts were first called to his attention he said he wouldn't retract unless Mrs. Meyer would retract not only what she had said about him but about McCarthy. He wouldn't retract a lie unless she retracted the documented truth, though he changed his mind after he read in the paper that what he had said was not only false but libelous. All of which lends point to Bishop Oxnam's query— would he have apologized at all, to anybody but the wife of a powerful newspaper publisher?

After that Mr. Velde's committee, the majority of which is composed of decent men, kept him for some months in hand. His kindred spirit, Donald Jackson of California, once sounded off against Bishop Oxnam, but the principal result of that episode was the exposure of the shabbiness and triviality of the material in the committee's "file" on the bishop. (Congressional committees seem to be the only people in the country who believe what they read in the *Daily Worker*.) And when the Un-American Activities Committee had to deal with the ex-Communists in New England, it seems to have been equitable in its treatment of those who were really ex. However, what some of its members think about the way it not only should but does operate was expressed by the same Donald Jackson when the committee heard the frightful news that Lucille Ball, to oblige her grandfather, had once registered as a Communist voter. "The committee," said Jackson, "is departing from its usual procedure so that fact may be separated from rumor, and no damage done Miss Ball." No harm would be done by a few more such departures from the usual procedure, so that no damage may be done to other innocent people less prominent than Lucille Ball.

But last November Velde broke away from his committee and put on a unilateral act which not merely did considerable harm to the prestige of his country, but interfered with some carefully laid plans of his party. After a couple of Republican defeats in Congressional by-elections something had to be done, and Attorney General Brownell decided to dig up the corpse of Harry Dexter White. The White case was

56

an old story—he had been dead five years—but the fullest possible use was to be made of it. Mr. Brownell himself sounded the keynote by declaring that White was known to be a Communist spy by ex-President Truman when he appointed him to high office. Brownell had got President Eisenhower's approval of the speech by the simple expedient of not telling him what he was going to say; and all the Republican forces were ready to exploit the break-through. (A few days later, to be sure, Brownell said that he had had no intention of impugning Mr. Truman's loyalty. If that is true the United States has an Attorney General who doesn't know what words mean and who, in spite of having been chairman of the Republican National Committee, is blankly ignorant of the political consequences of what he says and does. This takes some believing.)

At the moment, however, everything was fine. Brownell detonated his bomb; the White House press office was alerted to provide corroborative evidence; so was Governor Jimmy Byrnes of South Carolina; and what Brownell regarded as corroborative evidence from the FBI files was in his hands already. The Jenner committee was standing by to go into the case; Republican leaders had been provided with statements emphasizing the horror of this disclosure; and all this had been done from motives of the purest

57

patriotism—more in sorrow than anger, and without the faintest political taint.

But they had forgotten Velde. Without consulting his committee he promptly sent subpoenas—not invitations—to ex-President Truman, Supreme Court Justice Clark and Governor Byrnes, commanding them to come before him as well as Jenner and tell their stories. The motive was candidly disclosed by the committee's counsel to a Democratic member who wanted to know what was going on: this promised to be "a juicy hearing" and the Un-American Activities Committee had to "get into the act." After which it was somewhat difficult to represent the act as an objective nonpolitical enterprise, motivated only by zeal for the national security.

It probably never occurred to Velde that this attempt to haul up a former President of the United States to explain his conduct in office to a Congressional committee would have an effect abroad; but it did. Studious foreigners who had painfully learned about our doctrine of the separation of powers now found it apparently upset by this assertion of Congressional supremacy. Others were afraid the United States might be about to follow the example of some Latin-American republics, where the inauguration of a new administration is immediately followed by the flight of the outgoing president across the frontier—

or, if he can't get that far, to asylum in a friendly embassy.

Most foreigners found it somewhat ridiculous that Brownell and Velde were imputing sympathy with Communism to the man who has done more to stop Communism, the world around, than anybody else. And people who had grown used to looking to the United States for the leadership of the free world found it disturbing that our government seemed less interested in what was going on than in what was done (or not done, for the evidence was not conclusive) by a second-rank official who has been dead for years. Newspaper editorials asked, "Has America gone mad?" In friendly newspapers the answer was "No"; but the question had to be asked.

There were backfires at home too. The President stood up for Mr. Truman's loyalty and said he wouldn't have issued the subpoena; the Republican National Committee, whose approval Velde had once thought he had, pleaded with him to withdraw the subpoena. He didn't have to withdraw it, for Mr. Truman refused to respond to it, on constitutional grounds; so did Justice Clark; most unkindest cut of all, Jimmy Byrnes refused to respond. He had evidently taken seriously all the talk of State rights in the 1952 campaign, and he told Velde that Congress has no right to call a governor out of his state. Brownell and J. Edgar Hoover presented the case for the prosecution before the Jenner committee, Mr. Truman presented the case for the defense on the air; but nobody paid any attention to Velde.

I write as the first episode of this affair (Mr. Brownell promises us that there will be more) has come to an end; and it seems generally agreed that nobody came out of it too well. The President said that it was inconceivable that his predecessor had done what Brownell said he had done; but he had previously given Brownell, as a Democratic Congressman put it, "a hunting license without knowing what he wanted to shoot"; and that license is still valid so long as Brownell keeps off posted grounds; the President is not going to tell him how to run his department. Mr. Truman had a pretty good story to tell but told it badly, and further accused "the administration" of having embraced McCarthyism—a charge valid against some of its members, but not against the President himself, who can be the administration when he wants to be.

The Attorney General repeatedly assumed and declared the guilt of a man who had never been convicted of anything—prudently selecting a dead man who can't talk back, though he talked back vigorously when he was living; Mr. Brownell's reason, in addition to the known but inconclusive evidence, being

60

his own interpretation of FBI files which the public, properly, is not permitted to see; accordingly those who have seen them can interpret them as they may choose. The FBI has dossiers on millions of citizens; it frankly collects all kinds of evidence—rumor, gossip, guesswork, slander as well as facts; such few FBI reports as have been published show that much of this stuff is trivial, irrelevant or false. Mr. Brownell has now opened the way for it to be used for partisan purposes. Even the sacrosanct J. Edgar Hoover—a man exempt from the Congressional cross-examination that usually bedevils other witnesses—did not show up too well. He repeatedly insisted that he never evaluates the information he collects and then went on, in this case, to evaluate it; he made it clear that his evaluation differed from that of the President who was his superior officer; and he criticized Mr. Truman for following a procedure, in dealing with Harry White, that Hoover himself has said is the best way to handle suspects.

But the man who came off worst was Velde. He got not only a bad press but a practically unanimously bad press; Democratic papers damned him for what he had tried to do, Republican papers for interfering with what the Republican leadership was trying to do. So temperate a publication as the Washington *Star* called him a witless buffoon; Republican

61

leaders, in private, probably called him worst than that. As the *New Republic* put it, "The circus act in which the elephant was engaged was too profitable to be ruined by a clown."

All of which confirms the earlier impression that Mr. Velde is a useful man; but not to the people to whom he tries to be useful.

3.

Much to the general surprise, the investigations of Jenner's committee (as distinguished from the obiter dicta of its chairman) have probably done more good than harm. Its methods, shocking to people who had never seen it in action, were pallid to those who remembered McCarran. Jenner started off by declaring that "many hundreds" of teachers have been organized by the Communist party, in a secret underground operation that must be exposed and checked. He has failed to produce his hundreds, out of the eleven or twelve hundred thousand teachers in the United States, but he did turn up several dozen of whom some fifty or so refused to answer questions, taking refuge in the Fifth Amendment. I have no doubt that the great majority of these people had been Communists and that many of them were Communists still; some of those whom I saw, indeed, behaved as if they had gone through some sort of training school that taught them how to testify before a Congressional committee—talking as long as they could before they had to fall back on their constitutional rights.

The Fifth Amendment, providing that no man shall be compelled in any criminal case to be a witness against himself (this seems to be the only instance in which legal theory regards Congressional investigations as criminal prosecutions, which of course they are), was adopted for the benefit of the innocent, rather than the guilty, in memory of the kind of criminal prosecutions that were conducted in England in the seventeenth century and earlier. It seems highly probable that in this country it is much more often the guilty who have got the benefit. There can be a reason why somebody who was once a Communist (which, after all, is not a crime) and has got over it might take refuge in this protection—a reluctance to answer the questions, sure to follow, whose answers would betray one's friends and associates of those days. This reluctance is morally justifiable—always provided one is sure that their activities were not in fact subversive; and since most of these matters occurred fifteen or twenty years ago, when it was possible—as it hardly is now—to be a philosophical non-working Communist, that may well have been the case. But the law recognizes no such excuse; the only

63

refuge open for the ex-Communist who does not want to be an informer is to fall back behind the Fifth Amendment.

As for people who never were Communists, though they had been accused of so being, the way some of them feel was lately set forth by Dean Emeritus Paul Shipman Andrews of the Syracuse University Law School, who had served as counsel for a friend of his who had been accused by some ex-Communists of having attended Communist meetings fourteen years earlier (though they admitted that he might not have known they were Communist meetings). "There may be many different sets of circumstances," says Dean Andrews, "under which a man, knowing himself to be innocent of any wrong, might nevertheless wish to invoke the Fifth Amendment. Perhaps he cannot afford the heavy cost of defending himself, nor afford the time" (in case of a conflict of testimony which led to his indictment for perjury); "perhaps he dreads the strain of a possible prosecution, the humiliation, the black mark against him in the eyes of his friends even though he should be acquitted, the risk of being unjustly found guilty."

These considerations, of course, apply particularly to sensitive men. The lesson would seem to be that, during the present prevalence of Congressional investigations, no citizen can afford to be sensitive. "Why in the world," Dean Andrews goes on, "should an innocent man be presumed to be guilty of something, just because he uses, to protect himself, a right guaranteed by the United States Constitution?" Well, maybe he shouldn't be, but most people will so presume him. To fall back on the Fifth Amendment is any citizen's right, innocent or guilty; but in either case it is bad public relations.

There is another reason why some people I have heard of who never were Communists have sought this refuge: they were afraid that if they said they were not Communists some of these professional ex-Communist witnesses who play the circuit of the Congressional committees, as horse players go from one track to another, would denounce them as Communists, and then they would get indicted for perjury.

The fear seems plausible but is, I think, exaggerated. These wandering minstrels, as one target of the Jenner committee called them—I have no doubt that he was a Communist but that seems no reason to deprive him of credit for a pointed phrase—these people's testimony is generally accepted at face value by Congressional committees; but not always. No man has even been more relentlessly persecuted by a Congressional committee than Owen Lattimore by the Internal Security Committee under Senator McCarran. When they turned in their final report on the

Institute of Pacific Relations they made a recommendation which was practically a demand that Lattimore be indicted for perjury; and when Attorney General McGranery, in spite of his great obligations to McCarran, was a little slow about it, McCarran went after him again. So Lattimore was indicted.

Well, Lattimore himself had said that *somebody* ought to be indicted for perjury. Professor Louis Budenz of Fordham University, best known and most popular with Congress of the wandering minstrels, had declared on oath that he knows that Lattimore is a Communist—though he had previously told other people (not on oath) a different story. Lattimore declared on oath that he is not a Communist and never was, and added that either he or Budenz was guilty of perjury. Eventually Lattimore was indicted, but not on the ground of that flat conflict of testimony. If he had been, Budenz could have been brought to the stand in court and cross-examined under oath— an ordeal which the McCarran Committee had spared him, as Congressional committees spare all "friendly" witnesses—a friendly witness being one who backs up what the committee is trying to prove. Somebody— either McGranery or McCarran—evidently felt that it would be unkind to do that to Budenz, and the evidence on that point was never even presented to the grand jury.

66

Instead, the grand jury chose to indict Lattimore on the ground that he knowingly lied when he denied that he was a sympathizer with or promoter of Communism. Such a charge, of course, is practically impossible either to prove or to disprove; and thanks to the publicity given these Congressional hearings, the burden of disproof is on the defendant. As Lattimore's lawyer said, this was "a charge so vague that it could be made a basis for trying anyone in public life who advocated any policy, or expressed any opinion, with which any future committee or prosecutor might disagree."

Note that to find him guilty of perjury the trial jury would have had not only to find that Lattimore's opinions supported and promoted Communism, but that he knew they did and knowingly lied when he denied it. (If Senator Taft had been tried for perjury for denying the accusation of the real-estate lobbyist that he was following the Communist line, a jury of landlords might well have found that his support of public housing was a following of that line, but would undoubtedly have acquitted him on the ground that he didn't know it. Taft, however, was not Lattimore, against whom a powerful Congressional committee and a large section of the press and radio had long been conducting a campaign.)

In due course Judge Youngdahl in District Court

threw out that count of the indictment—almost the only one that had any substance—on the ground that it violated the Sixth Amendment to the Constitution in that the accused was not informed of the nature and cause of the accusation against him; that it was not a concise and definite statement of the essential facts constituting the offense charged; and that it involved a speculative fathoming of the uncertainties of the human mind. But Attorney General Brownell, zealous to show that he was just as good as his predecessor McGranery (which would not be difficult), at once asked the Court of Appeals to reinstate this count of the indictment and others which Judge Youngdahl had thrown out; and there, at this writing, the matter rests.

The failure, however, of the grand jury to indict on the downright conflict of evidence between Lattimore and Budenz would suggest that the fear of innocent people who fall back on the Fifth Amendment that their liberty would be sworn away by the wandering minstrels is somewhat overdrawn. That amendment has protected some of the innocent, a good many of the guilty—and, inevitably, public opinion is almost certain to feel that anybody who takes refuge behind it is guilty. The kindhearted Senator McCarran has endeavored to remove that odium by proposing a law (not yet adopted) providing that nobody can be punished for testimony given against himself; he has immunity for himself though he can still be compelled to turn in his friends. Unfortunately there is a gimmick in that. Congress can grant immunity for offenses only against federal, not against state, laws. Many states have stringent anti-Communist laws; so a man might still convict himself on his own testimony. All right, you say, if he is a Communist? Well, maybe so, but that is not the way the Founding Fathers wrote it in the book.

There is another gimmick in Mr. McCarran's proposal. There is, or used to be, a similar law in New York State, aimed primarily at corrupt officials, giving a man immunity from prosecution on any evidence he provided against himself. But he was permitted to waive immunity, voluntarily subject himself to any perils he might let himself in for (if that is not in the McCarran proposal now, Congress would be likely soon to add it). And in New York, investigators very soon got into the habit of demanding that a man who appeared before them should waive immunity; anybody who did not might as well have gone into court and pleaded guilty so far as public opinion was concerned.

But to get back to the Jenner committee, from which this digression started. No doubt some of those who pleaded the Fifth Amendment in its hearings were innocent, no doubt most of them were not. Practically all of them had been fingered by the more reliable ex-Communists, and their performance in the hearings gave the New York school system legal reason for getting rid of some people it had long wanted to get rid of, for valid reasons—well-grounded doubts of their loyalty—which did not meet the requirements of the law. As for Jenner's purge of United Nations employees, that involves not only complex loyalty questions but the problem of whether the United Nations is a part of the United States Government and under the authority of Congress. The rest of the world thinks not; but these investigations—in which Jenner and McCarthy are now competing—will certainly encourage the people who want to get the United Nations out of the United States and the United States out of the United Nations.

In the Harry White affair the Republican leadership had apparently regarded Jenner as more dependable than either Velde or McCarthy; which went to Jenner's head. He promptly indicated that he thought his jurisdiction extended to Canada, and persuaded (or scared) the State Department into backing up his demand that he be allowed to examine Igor Gouzenko, the former code clerk in the Russian embassy in Ottawa whose defection began the exposure of Communist spying in North America. The Canadian government, with a tolerance which our government would hardly reciprocate (since a Canadian investigation on American soil would provide no publicity for American politicians), said that Jenner could send up his agents to talk to Gouzenko, but under conditions which Jenner found unacceptable. Whether Jenner or the Canadian government is sovereign in Canada, at this writing, is still in dispute; but I can guess who will win.

But the affair had a much more serious aspect than this. It was not clear whether the Jenner committee was acting on its own motion or as an agency of the Chicago *Tribune,* which had long been conducting a compaign against the Canadian Minister of External Affairs, Mike Pearson. A female wandering minstrel, Elizabeth Bentley, had a couple of years earlier given testimony before the Jenner committee (then under McCarran's chairmanship) reflecting on Pearson; the testimony had never been made public, but the *Tribune* darkly hinted at it, in language which made it seem worse than it appears to have been. When Robert Morris, counsel for the Jenner committee, was asked about this he replied, "No comment." But there was plenty of comment north of the border, where members of Parliament and newspapers from one end of Canada to the other exploded in fury at what they called the vicious smear against Pearson and an attempt to blackmail the Canadian government. Where-upon Morris changed his tune and declared that no attack on Pearson was or ever had been contemplated.

But in the meantime a more or less professional anti-Communist writer in New York, on good terms with the committee, had made a speech to the Women's National Republican Club declaring that Pearson had consistently sabotaged American efforts to expose Russian intrigue, and quoting Elizabeth Bentley as saying that during the war, when Pearson was in Washington, he was used as a source of information by one of Miss Bentley's fellow spies. Charitably (or prudently) the speaker added that maybe Pearson didn't know he was being used.

It was widely believed in Canada that this information had been leaked to the speaker by the committee—something which the history of Congressional committees investigating Communism made plausible enough. Of course, among Americans who knew Mike Pearson, the universal reaction was "Who on earth would believe that he would do anything to help Communism?" Well, one man could—the man who called George Marshall a living lie and an eager front for traitors—Senator Jenner. One newspaper could—the Chicago *Tribune,* which three days before Pearl Harbor published to the world (including Hitler, who luckily didn't believe it) the plans by which we would fight a war if we had to fight a war. Men who themselves were so indifferent to national interests could easily believe that other men are as indifferent as they are.

And once again the national interest of the United States was gravely harmed by this attack on the Foreign Minister of our closest and most necessary ally—the national interest, and the international interest of the Atlantic alliance. For this coincided with Senator McCarthy's proposal to get American prisoners out of China by cutting off all aid to England, our next closest and most necessary ally. Stirring up suspicion and ill feeling among the three nations which are the core of the Atlantic alliance can tend only to the isolation and weakening of the United States. That happens also to be the principal objective of the Soviet government; but they have an obvious motive, and a reasonable one from the Soviet point of view. Jenner and McCarthy seem to have helped out the objective of the Soviet government, in the name of anti-Communism, from no motive except their own publicity and their own power.

4.

In due course the churches came in for attention—though all the chairmen loudly declared that they were not attacking the churches, still less religion as such, but only exposing individual clergymen who were Communists. To no one's surprise, it appeared that as usual their definition of a Communist is a man who wants reforms; a minister who believes that Christianity implies some endeavor to improve conditions here below instead of a single-minded concentration on preparation for the next world must be a Communist. That is, if he is a Protestant, or in some cases a Jew. There are many Catholic priests who labor earnestly for social reforms; it is probably a tribute to the power of their Church that no Congressional committee has attacked them, for the record of the committees would indicate that it is due to no hesitations on principle.

The Jews, so far, have been hit with only a few sideswipes; but the Protestants have taken a terrific beating. A wandering minstrel named Joseph Zack Kornfeder, who has testified before many committees on many subjects, told the Un-American Activities Committee that six hundred Protestant ministers were Communists and several thousand more were fellow travelers. He named a few names, whose bearers are now under investigation by ecclesiastical authorities. Mr. Kornfeder's qualifications as an authority on Protestantism today appear to consist in the fact that he was a Communist twenty years ago. A still more horrendous story however was told by J. B. Matthews—an ex-wandering minstrel, among many other

74

things, who now appears to have a job with the Hearst papers and was for about a minute staff director of McCarthy's committee. Matthews used to be a Methodist missionary; I trust that the heathen derived benefit from his ministrations, since it is not clear that anybody else ever has. Twenty years ago he was attacking the Protestant churches because they were liberal and thus (according to Matthews) backing the leadership of business reaction; some clergymen even spoke favorably of that (according to Matthews) reactionary big-business outfit, the Roosevelt administration. Last summer he published a magazine article attacking the Protestant clergy because they are liberal and thus backing Communism. "The largest single group supporting the Communist apparatus in the United States today is composed of Protestant clergymen," the article began. Ten pages later it said that "the vast majority of American Protestant clergymen are loyal to the free institutions of this country," but seven thousand of them have been "drawn into the network of the Communist conspiracy." Matthews named ninety-five; quite a number of them turned out to be dead, most of the others were known as liberal reformers. But to the all-or-nothing mind the liberal reformer is the worst man in the world. You may attack him from the Communistoid or the Fascistoid standpoint or—as many have done—from

75

both in succession; but to this type of mind the liberal reformer is wrong—and the more successful the wronger.

It appears that a good many clergymen had signed petitions in favor of liberal social reforms which they favored, reforms which the Communists professed to favor too. The reverend gentlemen would certainly have been wiser to look more closely into the origins of some of these petitions; but all this falls somewhat short of Matthews' sweeping assertions.

That magazine article cost him his job with the McCarthy committee—through no fault of McCarthy's. Later, in a broadcast, Matthews admitted that he could not personally under oath name fifteen Protestant clergymen who are Communists, or any who is a Communist spy; but he believed on information from others that there were at least a handful, and he stuck to his story that there are seven thousand or more who have bowed the knee to Baal and are serving Communism. The Methodist Bishop Lord has suggested that these are probably men who support public housing, fight for civil rights and believe in world peace. It would certainly be rash to assert that there are no Protestant ministers who are Communists, but, over all, Matthews seems to be as wrong now as he was twenty years ago when he was on the other side of the argument.

A far more respectable figure, Mr. Archibald Roosevelt, is just as concerned as Matthews about the implications of the "social gospel." He told the Un-American Activities Committee that "a great many of our ministers are not rendering the proper service to God, which is helping the individual man or woman in his or her personal problems. Their duty is to save souls, not to save forms of government or advocate alien causes." Is such a matter as, for instance, decent housing for the poor, with which many clergymen of all faiths have been concerned, an alien cause? Of Mr. Roosevelt's personal uprightness and patriotism there can be no question; but there seems some reason to question his judgment when he says that "only believers in tyranny or those who have committed shameful actions start the cries of 'witch hunt,' 'book burning,' 'freedom of speech,' 'academic freedom,' 'freedom of the press,' and so forth, whenever an investigation is started by the Congress."

Note the "only." No doubt some discreditable persons have raised these cries, but plenty of other people have raised them too; book burning indeed has been ill spoken of by the President of the United States. The outcry in favor of freedom of speech and the press was started a long time ago, by the men who founded this republic. Mr. Roosevelt says he has "documentary and testamentary proof" that there

77

was a deep-laid plot, which has been quite successful, to poison the minds of unsuspecting and fine people in furtherance of the Communist programs. There certainly was such a plot; but it does not follow that everybody who disagrees with Mr. Roosevelt about the social gospel, or about the value of the liberties guaranteed by the Constitution, has been a victim of it. In these matters it might be well to preserve a little sense of proportion.

But to your impassioned patriot a sense of proportion is as subversive as a dispassionate weighing of the evidence. Some years ago, when McCarthy was making his first attacks on the State Department, I ventured to suggest in a broadcast that these were merely accusations, so far; we had better wait and see if the evidence justified convictions. Whereupon an infuriated citizen, apparently a man of standing in his community, wrote me, "We cannot wait for convictions; what we want is confessions." But suppose there is nothing to confess? That is no problem in Russia or any other totalitarian country; they get the confessions anyway. But this republic has not been operated on that principle, so far.

Some people apparently would have it so operated; when you are fighting Communism, they think, anything goes. Whether civil liberties should apply to people who, if they got into power, would destroy

78

civil liberties is an old problem, which was raised in many countries, and by Hitler's activities as well as Stalin's. The conclusion usually reached has been that they ought to apply to everybody; subversion should be kept down, but by other means.

The President seemingly thinks otherwise—or did, at least, when he made his campaign speech at Milwaukee in October 1952. "The Bill of Rights contains no grant of privilege for a group of people to join together to destroy the Bill of Rights. A group like the Communist conspiracy, dedicated to the ultimate destruction of all civil liberties, cannot be allowed to claim civil liberties as its privileged sanctuary." In other words, the Bill of Rights not only should not apply to Communists, which is a matter of opinion, but does not, which is a matter of fact. Has the President read it? I can find nothing in its language that says, or even implies, that any citizen or group of citizens is excepted from its guarantees. If the Constitution is to apply to everybody but Communists, pretty soon it might apply to everybody but Socialists, or Jehovah's Witnesses, or Episcopalians, or Democrats—anybody whom the majority didn't like and chose to regard as subversive. To prevent the majority from doing anything that may suit its whim of the moment is precisely the reason why we have a Constitution.

But is not Communism a deadly danger? Certainly it is, in Russia, and as operated from Russia; certainly the Communist party in this country is dedicated to the service of Russian imperialism. But such danger as it presents is a matter of espionage and sabotage, and if the FBI is half as good as we hope it is, it ought to be able to take care of that. In 1932 Communism was a more serious danger; the economic system of the United States had broken down, the governmental system sometimes seemed on the verge of breakdown. People used to ask helplessly, "Do you think there is going to be a revolution?"—not as if they either wanted a revolution or were resolutely determined not to have one, but as if there was nothing they could do about it. I do not think there was any serious danger of a revolution then (though greater men disagreed with me); if there had been one the Communists could not have started it, nor do I think they could have got control of it. Still their alternative to collapse had some plausibility—till it began to fade before a new administration, new policies, the beginnings of recovery.

The danger was greater in the "intellectual" world than elsewhere, then and for a few years afterward. I do not believe it was ever as great as represented by Alistair Cooke in *A Generation on Trial* or by Peter Viereck in *Shame and Glory of the Intellec-*

80

tuals; still Communism had its attraction for bright young people who came out of college and couldn't find jobs. Most of the cases that have lately been heard before Congressional committees had their beginnings in the thirties, and many of them had their end there. When the bright young people got jobs, most of them were cured; it was the Roosevelt recovery that killed the Communist danger. Of those who were not cured then, many were cured by the Hitler-Stalin treaty and most of the rest of them by the subsequent behavior of the Russian government. The fellow traveler, by now, is a species almost extinct.

As for the Communist party, the headlong decline in its membership is no doubt due in part to people going underground, but there is ample evidence that many of them are giving up and quitting—either from fear or because they have (very belatedly) realized what they had got into. Whatever the reason, that hard core is shrinking fast; as Professor Caughey of U.C.L.A. has remarked, never in history were so many thrown into panic by so few.

I am not unmindful of the fact that Mr. J. Edgar Hoover tells us each year that Communism is a greater danger than it ever was before—which, if true, is a serious reflection on Mr. Hoover and his organization, whose business it is to root it out. But I am

81

not too much alarmed; these statements are usually made before the Appropriations Committee, when he is asking for (and always getting) more money for his agency. I have had some experience in government, and much observation of it, and I cannot recall that the head of any agency, appearing before the Appropriations Committee, ever underestimated the need for his services.

Yet the Communist party, tiny and dwindling as it is, serves one useful purpose in the minds of many of our public men: it provides them with a cover for attacks on liberalism and progressive reforms—attacks which might have less hope of success if they had to be made honestly, out in the open; and, quite as important, it enables them in denouncing Communism to find the road to publicity and power. It has been quite a meal ticket for some of our statesmen whose natural gifts might not otherwise have carried them very far; and not merely for statesmen. There are a good many little organizations around the country—most of them fly-by-night but one or two fairly influential—which have made of fighting Communism (or rather what they choose to call Communism) a lucrative business; I sometimes suspect that the people engaged in that business are more numerous than the Communists. From the standpoint of all these gentlemen, in office or out, if Communism did not exist, it would be necessary to invent it. (A few of those organizations are sincere and effective; but far from all.)

But it does exist, and I shall no doubt be accused of underestimating it. Its intentions are certainly as evil as possible; it has tried to infiltrate the churches, the schools, the labor unions; worst of all, it has tried to infiltrate the government, with some success. How much success?

Plenty, if you believe a report issued in September 1953 by Mr. Jenner's Internal Security Committee of which the Republican National Committee, and one of McCarthy's oil millionaries, have distributed hundreds of thousands of copies. "Literally scores of agents penetrated the United States government. They hired each other. They promoted each other. They raised each other's salaries. They vouched for each other's loyalty and protected each other when exposure threatened. They often had common living quarters. There was a group that played handball together." (The relevance of this particular piece of infamy is not clear.) "Except in a few cases all of these agents escaped punishment; and some, in positions of influence, continued to flourish even after their exposure." But the past is prologue, says Senator Jenner (who has evidently read the inscription on the front of the Archives Building); some of these people, unexposed because undiscovered, are spying still. The committee does not know who they are or what they are up to, but Elizabeth Bentley, an ex-Communist and thus by definition infallible, says there are some still around (or at least were eight years ago). This penetration, says the committee, extended to "top-level policy and operating positions"; and some of these people were "responsible for extensive perversion of policy that consequently caused the loss of thousands of American lives."

A formidable indictment. But I trust it will not be regarded as subversive to take a look at it and try to figure how much truth there is in it (there is undoubtedly some, and any is too much) and how much elastic inference. In the first place, this is not news. To get a good story the committee had to go into the reprint business; the evidence here reported is an anthology of testimony (mostly by ex-Communists) before various committees for eight years past. All that is new—and even that is not very new—is the committee's conclusions. That these people helped to get jobs for one another, promoted one another, is undoubtedly true; also, in the main, that "little was done by the executive branch to interrupt them in their ascent, until Congressional committees brought forth to light the facts of the conspiracy."

But the committees seem to have brought forth

84

something more than the facts. Granted that the executive branch was sometimes lax in taking action on real evidence, in other cases the evidence was open to serious question except by those to whom the word of an ex-Communist is like the counsel of Ahithophel, which was as if a man had inquired at the oracle of God. Of the scores the committee mentions it names twenty-odd; two of them are dead and all but one of the others are out of the government. If one is still in the government, and some others who have left hold honorable positions, it is conceivably because other people do not hold the same view of evidence as Congressional committees. And while the record shows that in such differences of opinion the committees are sometimes right, they are perhaps not always so.

All these people, says the committee, have been identified as Communists. "Identified," in Congressional idiom, means that somebody has said they are Communists. Thirty-six who appeared before the Jenner committee, and others who appeared before other committees, took refuge behind the Fifth Amendment and refused to say whether they were or not; in such cases the presumption that the identification had been correct is, if not absolutely conclusive, certainly very strong. One or two of them have admitted it, though denying any subversive activities; one man, protected

85

by the statute of limitations, coolly admitted that he had been just as great a scoundrel as his accusers maintained. But there were a number of others who indignantly denied the accusation, and no corroborative evidence appeared to back up the wandering minstrels who accused them. This was true of the three most important men on the list; Harry White (against whom there was some evidence in Chambers' pumpkin papers) is now dead, another has left the government (of his own accord) and the third is still employed by superiors who, after all this uproar, have investigated him more thoroughly than the committee ever did.

More curious is the case of a man mentioned not only in this report but in a supplement issued three weeks later. If you believe Elizabeth Bentley, he was a very evil man indeed—about the worst of the lot. But he is a peaceful Republican businessman now— out of the government, and he got out of his own accord. He had been promoted twice in the government service, with increases in salary; but he quit, the record shows, "because he was unwilling to accept a reduction in rank and thus give up some of these benefits." A strange story. Here, according to the official senatorial theory, was a dedicated revolutionary, whose whole life was devoted to the business of undermining the United States for his masters in Moscow. He was in a position where he could do, and

according to the official theory was doing, considerable damage; yet he quit, threw up this golden opportunity, practically betrayed the Communist cause,
rather than take a pay cut. Something here seems
out of focus.

But to any skepticism your Red-hunter has what
he thinks is a crushing and complete rejoinder—Alger Hiss. Because Hiss's friends long believed he was
innocent, and a jury found him guilty, anybody who
is accused must be guilty—and indeed people whom
nobody has got around to accusing yet. There is no
answer to this argument, except that it makes no
sense. How many of our fellows citizens will feel that
that is a serious objection time will discover.

But to return to the Jenner committee. The chro-
nology of its report raises some questions too. All
this wickedness that has been publicly reported took
place years ago, but the committee says it is still going on. It says so because Miss Bentley was told by
one of her Soviet contacts that there were two other
spy rings in the government with which she had no
connection and which have not yet been exposed.
When was she told? She says she quit the party in
1945 and presumably had no contacts after that; certainly she would have had none after 1948, when she
began testifying in public. If this is still going on, no
evidence of that has been produced.

87

You would expect the Jenner committee to say it is all over. Almost all these dozens of people came into the government (along with a million or so other people) in the Roosevelt administration—though the first and apparently the most efficient organizer was in there under Coolidge, and some alleged skulduggery in the State Department which McCarthy reported in 1953, with the clear implication that it happened in 1953, had actually occurred (if it ever occurred at all) in 1928. Still, most of them certainly came in under Roosevelt; and you might have expected the Jenner committee, with its heavy Republican-Republicrat majority, to say that these terrible things that happened under Democratic administrations could not happen any more now that Republicans are on guard in the executive branch. Not at all; they say it is still going on. . . . But if it were not going on, people might feel that there was no more need for a Senate Internal Security Committee.

The main point, however—granting that there certainly were Communists in government, and that their intentions were as evil as possible—the main point is, what did they accomplish? Terrible things, according to the Jenner committee: "Policies and programs laid down by members of the Soviet conspiracy are still in effect within our government." No examples are given, so the reader can set down any policy he

88

doesn't like as the work of enemy agents. The committee's further statement that the penetration extended to top-level policy and operating positions can be justified only by an extremely elastic definition of *top-level*. Harry White was close to top-level, but he was about the only one; and until the Attorney General tells us the evidence that persuaded him, there is no convincing proof that White served any government but his own.

But undoubtedly the Communists did some damage; if they were not top-level men they were often industrious assistants to top-level men, in the executive departments and on Congressional committees. The report is doubtless right in saying that their work was "guiding research and preparing memoranda on which basic American policies were set, writing speeches for cabinet officers, influencing Congressional investigations, and drafting laws." Such "assistance," given to an unsuspecting superior, might have a considerable indirect influence on policy; yet the committee cites no such influence on policies that were actually adopted.

So with espionage. "How many priceless American secrets have been conveyed to Moscow through the American Communist underground," says the committee, "will never be known"; so you can let your imagination run wild. Undoubtedly these eager beavers got a good deal of information, and to a good intelligence service any information is valuable; yet there has been no evidence that any of it was priceless. The one thing we do know is that the one priceless secret that was stolen—how to make the atomic bomb go off—was not stolen by any of these people but by an army sergeant and a scientist working for an allied government. The papers found in Whittaker Chambers' pumpkin (Chambers had not passed them on, but that is not the fault of the man who took them) would have enabled a foreign power to break the State Department code; and two of them, according to Sumner Welles, would, if disclosed, have been dangerous to the national interest. But whether the Russians actually got anything good from that source will, as the committee truly says, never be known.

According to the voluble Miss Bentley, they got all kinds of information out of the armed services during the war. If we had been fighting the Russians this leakage might have been disastrous; but we happened then to be on the same side (a fact usually forgotten), and the discoveries of which she seems proudest had been officially told to the Russian government long before. All this is no excuse whatever for the intention of the spies, but it may bring into some proportion what they actually succeeded in accomplishing.

If the Jenner committee wants us to believe that Communists were responsible for baneful policies still in force, it had better say what policies, and who put them over, when and how. That use of them "caused the loss of thousands of American lives" rests on the dogma, firmly held (or at least firmly asserted) by the Internal Security Committee, that Communists controlled the Institute of Pacific Relations; that it in turn controlled the State Department, and that the State Department sold China down the river and thereby brought on the Korean war. This belief is held by many people, probably more fervently than they believe in the principles of their religion; but there are few if indeed any competent historians among them.

All these investigations have certain characteristics in common—the elastic inference, the doctrine of guilt by association, the reliance on the testimony of the touring company of ex-Communists that makes the rounds of the committees—"people," as the Washington *Star* once described them, "whose only claim to credibility is that they used to belong to a society of liars." Sometimes certainly they have told the truth; sometimes, just as certainly, they have indulged in the inventive imagination.

This is an old story; with McCarthy, something new has been added. His vindictiveness, if not less

91

than McCarran's, is certainly of a different type. Mc-Carran used to grab his victim by the throat and shake him till he had got everything out of him; McCarthy seems to lose interest after he has got all out of him that would do any good to McCarthy. But he is a master of the obscene innuendo, and he has more effrontery in direct attack than any of his fellow saviors of the nation. None of them, when Jim Wechsler had optimistically supposed he could show evidence of his anti-Communism by producing an attack on him by the *Daily Worker,* would have thought of suggesting, as McCarthy did, that he probably wrote it himself as a cover for his nefarious activities.

McCarthy's committee differs from all the others in that it seems to have little appetite for publication. In its first eight months of existence it issued only one report—on foreign trade with China—though several others were said to be in the works. McCarthy gets his effects on the front page, rather than by anything set down in print where readers could critically examine it. And if yesterday's front-page story blows up today, there is always today's front-page story to bury the refutation. It is a question how many people would recognize that it has blown up anyway; as Joe Alsop has written, "One of his great assets is that his supporters have the true mark of the fanatic— they are not interested in facts. The endless exposures

of McCarthy's endless untruths do not affect them."
He has also, Alsop adds, got the support of a great
deal of money—which is even truer now than when
it was written. Already in the fall of 1952 he had
quite a lot; his famous broadcast attacking the "Communist influences" around Stevenson was paid for
pretty largely by the old America First crowd. When
I listened to that broadcast the past rose before me
like a dream—a past I thought had been buried seven
years before. I was reminded of another rabble-rous-
ing broadcaster in another republic, who was taken up
by rich men and conservative politicians because they
thought they could use his talent for publicity against
a middle-of-the-road government and then throw him
over when he had served their purpose. But when he
once got to the eminence to which he had been climb-
ing, he threw them over when they had served his
purpose. When I heard the applause for McCarthy
that night an echo of memory seemed to give it an
undertone—*Sieg Heil! Sieg Heil! Sieg Heil!*

Whether McCarthy expects to become President I
would not know; but it looks that way. The liberal
Republican theory is that he could have a chance of
it only if the Eisenhower administration is a failure—
something that nobody will know for a couple of
years. In the meantime, the President has certainly
not done much to stop him. To be sure, he no longer

quite seems to bestride this petty world like a colossus, as he did in early spring of 1953 when he was running through the State Department—its information service particularly—virtually without interference. Most of the foreign overestimates of his power, and the talk of the "reign of terror," date from those days. But he is still, at this writing, somebody of consequence; his latest target is the Army, where he grossly misinterpreted a classified document put out to inform our troops about the nature of the enemy. Classified; but McCarthy airily declared, "I declassified it." It had been classified only as "restricted," the lowest degree of privacy, and it might seem that its declassification could hardly do any harm to the national interest—though *Pravda* used it as evidence that McCarthy was exposing the war preparations of the Joint Chiefs of Staff, and the incident led to the transfer to another job of an apparently competent chief of Army Intelligence for the crime of disagreeing with Louis Budenz. In any case McCarthy had no right to declassify it. A trivial incident, but suggesting that he regards himself as *legibus solutus*, like the Roman Emperors—not bound by the laws. And there is another indication that in his mind there is one law for McCarthy and another for everybody else. In his investigation of the Government Printing Office he discovered that a few of its employees had been buying lottery tickets—which in his opinion was a peril to the national security. These people might have access to secret information (though there was no evidence of it, and the likelihood that they had was infinitesimal), and their gambling losses might subject them to blackmail by enemy agents.

McCarthy has plenty of access to secret information; he often goes to the races and loses money there; but this evidently entails no peril to the national security. However, there has been testimony that he is often accompanied by men who are under obligation to him and cash checks for him if he fails to pick a winner.

Last spring Peter Viereck, convinced that McCarthy was only an "inflated balloon ogre" (the sort of underestimate that has enabled him to get where he is), thought that the balloon could be pricked and popped. "The right person to pop McCarthy by public refutation must be a fellow-Republican so beyond suspicion in the eyes of America that no slander can stick to him. The person who best meets that specification is Dwight Eisenhower. Unless," Viereck went on, "the new Republican administration restrains or pops this specter, it will be guilty of flagrant moral evasion"—a most opprobrious phrase, to describe a natural desire for party harmony. Since then the

President has "restrained" McCarthy four times, but he has not popped him; if I may be pardoned for a simile from the history of a great general and a great citizen, McCarthy has had his Malvern Hill but not his Gettysburg. The President has shown that he can restrain McCarthy when he wants to, but all of the four occasions when he has wanted to were special instances, with little relation to the general problem of McCarthyism.

The first was his insistence on sending Chip Bohlen as Ambassador to Moscow—a man whom he knew well and knew to be the best qualified for perhaps our most important diplomatic post. The President put that over, in spite of the fact that Bohlen, before the Senate Foreign Relations Committee, had refused to say that Yalta was a treasonable betrayal of American interests; but the senators who put it over for him seem to have warned him that he had better not make any more controversial appointments. When the appointment of Mildred McAfee Horton, to everybody's amazement, proved to be controversial, the administration turned tail and ran.

The President also refused to permit McCarthy to interfere with the Central Intelligence Agency, of whose importance and delicacy he was well aware; it can be hoped that he will equally appreciate the importance, and in some respects the delicacy, of the

International Information Agency now that it is no longer under the State Department but directly responsible to the White House. McCarthy has not left much of it but wreckage, but there are people living in the rubble who would still like to do a good job, if anybody will give them a chance.

The third instance in which the President moved against McCarthy, but so indirectly that McCarthy could deny that it was a move against him at all, was a case that was bound to rouse the ire of an administration which, if not the most religious, is certainly the most devout we have ever had. Just after the celebrated J. B. Matthews had been appointed staff director for McCarthy's committee there appeared his magazine article saying that the Protestant clergy were the largest single group supporting the Communist apparatus. McCarthy said he had known nothing about this beforehand, and I suspect that for once he was telling the truth. Why should he have known about it? The offense was appointing a man with Matthews' record in the first place. Anyway, the three Democratic members of his committee denounced this as a shocking and unwarranted attack, and one of the four Republicans, Mr. Potter, seemed to sympathize with them. By the next week Potter had apparently been brought around, for the four Republicans voted that McCarthy had full authority to hire and fire staff

97

members; whereupon the three Democrats resigned from the committee.

The day before they resigned, however, the President had had a message from three prominent clergymen—a Catholic, a Protestant and a Jew—declaring that Matthews' attack had been unjustified and deplorable; and the President promptly replied that generalized and irresponsible attacks on any group portray contempt for the principles of freedom and decency and that it is even worse when such an attack tends to undermine the church. This was vague enough to give McCarthy an excuse for saying with injured innocence, "Who, me?" But everybody knew who. A couple of hours later Matthews' resignation was announced, though there is good reason to believe that it had come in earlier and had been forced by the senators rather than by the President.

The final instance (earlier in point of time) was the celebrated book-burning episode. It is of course true that very few books had actually been burned and only at one or two of the State Department's overseas libraries; but the term had become a synonym for the removal, by whatever method, of books that might seem to contain what the Japanese police used to call dangerous thoughts, or that, whatever they contained, were the work of "suspect" authors. Accordingly, many hearts leaped up when the President unexpectedly interpolated into a talk at Dartmouth, "Don't join the book burners. Don't think you are going to conceal thoughts by concealing evidence that they ever existed." Naturally McCarthy said, "He couldn't have meant me; his own administration has been removing the books" (scared into so doing, of course, by McCarthy). And indeed the President, asked about it at his next news conference, refused to say that he had meant McCarthy or anybody else; he never, he said, talks personalities.

Then why the outburst at Dartmouth? Well, it seems to have been the instinctive reaction of a decent man, before he had had time to get advice, to something scandalous that he had not known was going on till Mike Pearson told him. But the Canadian Minister of External Affairs is a busy man; he cannot always be around to tell the President of the United States something that he could have read in the papers, if he read the papers. (More than once, at his news conferences, the President has shown himself unaware of news that had been on all the front pages.)

All's well that ends well. The President eventually approved a very sane and sensible directive about books in American libraries overseas; he went further and gave his personal *nihil obstat* to inclusion in those libraries of the works of Dashiell Hammett, who has thus attained a peak of official endorsement not reached by any other American author. But whether the episode was a setback to McCarthy is far from clear.

Much more important, potentially—though it is merely a resistance to McCarthy's invasion of the executive field, not any disapproval of McCarthyism on principle—is something just undertaken as I write; whether or not it will have been carried through, and carried through successfully, you may know by the time this book is published. The only report the McCarthy committee has so far issued deals with trade with China—especially British trade, which, in so far as the British government can assure it, is entirely in nonstrategic materials. As usual with McCarthy, there was a small nubbin of fact—distorted, inflated and used as the foundation for a superstructure of inference and suspicion. On the basis of that, McCarthy practically declared war on England, demanding that we sink all British ships engaging in the China trade. When he found that nobody was following him in this one-man crusade, he cut down his demand and merely proposed that we give England not one cent more aid, military or economic.

Here, the administration apparently decided that they had to resist him. Harold Stassen's Foreign Operations Administration got out a booklet stating the facts on East-West trade and denouncing myths about

100

it; in accordance with standard procedure no myth-maker was named, but everybody knew who was meant. And McCarthy's colleague, Senator Wiley, followed this up with a vigorous speech, saying that the free nations were going to go on trading with China in nonstrategic goods whether we like it or not, and that we should not "ask the impossible" of our friends and demand that they stop it. All this seems to reflect a firm decision by the administration; whether it will still be firm when you read this, I cannot guess.

What did hurt McCarthy in the summer of 1953 was the withdrawal of all the Democrats from his committee and the refusal of any other Democrats to replace them—not to mention some indication that one of his Republicans, Mr. Potter, was becoming weary in well-doing. The faithful Karl Mundt still sticks to McCarthy like Friday to Robinson Crusoe; Everett Dirksen is around from time to time; but the committee, by now, is pretty much a one-man show—McCarthy.

This, however, doesn't worry him; losing the Democrats meant losing any claim to be making an impartial bipartisan investigation, but it also meant getting rid of three men who had occasionally intervened to get some fairness and accuracy in his hearings. Meanwhile his popular support seemed in no way diminished. The New York County chapter of the

101

Veterans of Foreign Wars gave him thirty thousand dollars to carry on his good work (not that he didn't have plenty of money already, but it helps to get more from so respectable a source); the Marine Corps gave him a Distinguished Flying Cross for "heroism and extraordinary achievement" on thirty combat missions, though four years earlier he himself had claimed only seventeen; and the Wall Street post of the American Legion gave him, believe it or not, its Bill of Rights Gold Medal for "exceptional protection and defense of our way of life." (*Whose* way of life? Well, his way may be fastened on us yet.)

And any slight political reverses he may have suffered will soon be forgotten, for he is to be rehabilitated—"brushed off and cleaned up," as Marquis Childs puts it—and used as the spearhead of the Republican senatorial campaign in 1954. This is astute strategy—ascribed by the Associated Press, which first reported the story, to Vice-President Nixon; for even if they cannot extract a promise from him (or trust it, if they did extract it) to lay off the executive departments now that they are headed by Republicans, the all-out attack on the "Truman-Acheson gang" might keep him too busy to bother with anybody else—at least till the election has been won. It was proved in the senatorial elections of 1950, and some of those of 1952, that it pays better to call your

102

opponents Communists, or soft on Communism, than to discuss the issues. Nineteen fifty-four also may be that kind of year; Senator Ferguson seems to think so. He is up for re-election and his prospects are uncertain; his denunciation of "radical eggheads" suggests that he feels that his best hope of victory lies in an attack on intelligence. Mr. Ferguson, of course, is a man of principle, but I doubt if his hostility to intelligence on principle is strong enough to lead him to attack it, or attack anything else, unless he felt that by so doing he would get votes. There will be plenty of other men running for office in the fall of 1954 who feel that way.

The President has said, with unquestionable sincerity, that he hopes Communism in government will not be an issue in next fall's election. Other men apparently hope and expect otherwise—the Attorney General, for instance; the chairman of the Republican National Committee; House Leader Charlie Halleck; above all, McCarthy himself, who said that that election will be a vote of confidence (or of no confidence) not in Eisenhower but in him and pointed that up by making it clear that Eisenhower's behavior on McCarthy's issue is far from satisfactory to McCarthy. No more of those unctuous references to "our great President Eisenhower"; the question of who is the top man is now out in the open.

Optimists will say that in coming out so plainly, and above all so soon, McCarthy has shown that he is getting too big for his pants. But they have said that before and they were wrong. Unless Congress passes a few miracles at this session it will be a great temptation to many men to fight the election of 1954 on the issue, not of what Eisenhower has done in 1954 or what Malenkov has done in 1954, but of what Harry White did or did not do ten years ago. There used to be a type of Southern blatherskite politician who, lacking a real issue, or lacking the character and ability that would enable him to get elected on real issues, nevertheless achieved public office by the pastime locally known as "hollering nigger." Men like that are happily fewer than they used to be; but it looks as if this fall there may be many men in the North, so respectable that it would be sheer blasphemy to call them blatherskites, who will count on getting elected by hollering Communist.

For such a campaign as this promises to be, McCarthy has unique talents; he can conduct (to quote Childs again) "a campaign of smear and innuendo, directed not only at the candidate but at members of his family"—something that men who regard themselves, correctly or not, as more respectable would hesitate to do. Against such tactics no retaliation is possible; nobody else could get down so low as McCarthy, even if anybody wanted to.

104

All in all, McCarthy seems to be about as formidable in fact, even if perhaps not in appearance, as he was at the beginning of 1953. He still has his mass following, impervious to facts; and he has, or soon will have, the support of many respectable men who feel that his value to his party outweighs any harm he may do to his, and their, country. They may be right—at least so long as he belongs to the party, and not it to him.

5.

Well, what do we do about all this? About McCarthy the ordinary citizen cannot do much if anything, unless he gets the Presidential nomination in 1956; and we won't know that for two years. The Senate could do something; it could examine the report of its own committee, and if it found that the evidence there justified expulsion, it could expel him. But it won't. General Eisenhower could have done something in the fall of 1952 merely by staying out of Wisconsin; even with his support, McCarthy ran at the tail end of the ticket. But Eisenhower was persuaded that the way for him to get support in Congress was to call for the election of all Republican candidates (had he but known! as the old-fashioned mystery writers used to say); so he not only let McCarthy campaign with him in Wisconsin, but made

105

his Milwaukee speech on McCarthy's issue and very much in McCarthy's language.

Once a senator is in, there is not much that a President can do about him—as President Roosevelt discovered in 1938 when he tried to defeat some of them for re-election. Even so, early in 1953 Eisenhower, who had won a tremendous personal victory when his party barely scraped through, might have done what so many of his followers were imploring him to do and used his prestige to go on record as disliking Mc-Carthyism—as, his friends say and as seems highly probable, he privately does. But he chose not to do so; to date, he seems content to stay within his perimeter defense and has not put up much of a fight to hold even such important outposts as some parts of the State Department.

Nor is there much the ordinary citizen can do about Congressional committees if he is haled before them. There may be limits on their investigative rights, but those rights can be delimited only by litigation which would be too long and costly for the average man. None of them has recently gone so far as the late J. Parnell Thomas, who once told a witness, "You have no rights except what this committee chooses to give you"; but the committee controls the procedure and has a dozen ways to oppress the witness, if it chooses. And even if he stands up well, and seems to have

106

made a good showing in his testimony, it is the committee which writes the eventual report and can slant it so as to give a very different impression.

But we can all do something to resist this general drive against the freedom of the mind. The first thing to remember is, Don't let them scare you. Arthur Sulzberger said recently that what bothered him was not the superzealot attackers so much as the lack of plain old-fashioned guts on the part of the people who give in to them. And it has been shown in a dozen places that if you stand up to them you can often stop them.

Not always and not finally, for it will be a very long time indeed before we are rid—if ever—of the kind of people who want to make other people think their way, or else stop thinking at all. But we can hold them in check, push them back—always remembering to keep an eye on them, always remembering that eternal vigilance is the price of liberty. Particularly the attacks on the schools can be checked, as they have been checked in many places. You are not going to cure the genuine Fascists who spearhead these attacks, but they get their support largely from the people who are ignorant and afraid; get rid of the ignorance and you get rid of a good deal of the fear. It is usually possible to educate a school board; indeed it is possible to educate a Legion post, and it has been done. There seems no logical necessity for local veterans organizations to fall into the hands of reactionaries, even though the major national organizations have done so; if local posts do so too, it is because the reactionaries work at it and most people don't.

In Hagerstown, Maryland, the few local believers in world government brought to town a play that advocated it. Some leading members of the Legion burst out with attacks on the play and some of the participants, but they had their facts wrong and were talked down. But even before that happened the local chapter of the Veterans of Foreign Wars had announced that they were just as much opposed to world government as the Legion (so am I, if that makes any difference) but that they were also opposed to "scare tactics"; they urged all citizens to go and see the play and make up their minds about it. Which is all that anyone could ask.

In Oregon, all the veterans got educated. There had been the usual sort of attacks on the schools; but the state commander of the American Legion, speaking for practically all the veterans' organizations, came to their support. If there is complaint about the schools, he said, the educational authorities should have the opportunity to clean house, or determine whether it was necessary to clean house, without being harassed by outside organizations. There, the veterans' societies had taken the trouble to find out what it was all about, and somebody had taken the trouble to help them. That could happen elsewhere, if somebody would only take the trouble.

Such education, of course, could be a two-way process. It was the opposite direction which the President emphasized in his talk to the United Churchwomen at Atlantic City in the fall of 1953. A small group, he said, had come to him to complain about certain things in our public-school system. "And I asked this group one question only. . . . Have you taken the trouble to find out what is the philosophy of these people to whom you are entrusting the most precious possession you have—your children? If you join the ranks of the critics and say that these teachers are not doing a good job, then why haven't you done your part of the job?—brought them in, talked to them, to see whether you can either straighten them out, or get ones of whom you can approve."

The value of such a straightening-out process would seem to depend on two things—whether the parents have an informed and intelligent opinion as to what the schools ought to accomplish, so that they can competently evaluate the philosophy of the teachers; and whether, if they fail to straighten the teachers out, they would leave any action to the school board or other duly constituted authority after public discussion, or would use whatever extraofficial political or economic power the parents might possess to "get ones of which they approve." That the teachers might conceivably straighten the parents out was apparently unthinkable to the President. No doubt his intention was to promote a more general citizen interest in education, but his language could be misinterpreted as a license to every pressure group to put the heat on.

The colleges are in a tougher spot. Some of their organizations displayed a visionary optimism about the educative possibilities of Congressional investigations; and what happens in an individual college usually depends on the courage of its president and the intelligence of its trustees and alumni. (It is one of the facts of life, painful though it may be, that courage comes easier the bigger the endowment. Harvard, Columbia and Chicago would probably have stood up anyway, in view of their traditions; but they needed less propping than some others.) Yet none of the things that Jenner and Velde actually did lived up to their thundering in the index; indeed the investigations, and the big talk that preceded them, may have done some good in compelling the colleges to do some hard thinking about what they had that was worth fighting for.

As for the general attack on freedom of thought,

110

it comes in such manifold form that it requires more kinds of defense than can be listed here; and sometimes the defense will be in vain. When a magazine fiction editor is fired because another editor, unknown to him, bought a nonfiction article which evoked some protest; when an actress is dropped from a radio program because a couple of dozen telephone calls, probably stimulated, scared the sponsor—why, in such cases there is nothing much you can do about it except to regret that there are so many cowards in the world. But sometimes the defense is successful; and you never get anywhere unless you stand up and fight.

This was stated in the fall of 1953, at the dinner of the Four Freedoms Foundation, in language so much to the point that I shall not venture to try to improve on it:

> The good life is not possible without freedom. But only the people, by their will and by their dedication to freedom, can make the good life come to pass. We cannot leave it to the courts alone, because many of the invasions of these freedoms are so devious and so subtle that they cannot be brought before the courts.
>
> The responsibility for these freedoms falls on free men. And free men can preserve them only if they are militant about freedom. We ought to get angry when these rights are violated, and make

ourselves heard until the wrong is righted. . . . There are times when the defense of freedom calls for vigorous action. This action may lead to trouble, and frequently does. Effective effort to preserve freedom may involve discomfort and risk. It takes faith, unselfishness and courage to stand up to a bully; or to stand up for a whole community when it has been frightened into subjection. But it has to be done, if we are to remain free.

We have to start wherever we can—in the family, the lodge, the business community, the union, our local government, party, church—and work outward; asserting, demanding, insisting that the most unpopular persons are entitled to all the freedoms, to fundamental fairness. Almost always, the issues are raised over unpopular people or unpopular causes. In the cause of freedom, we have to battle for the rights of people with whom we do not agree; and whom, in many cases, we may not like. These people test the strength of the freedoms which protect all of us. If we do not defend their rights, we endanger our own.

Since the foregoing was said by Harry S. Truman, I suppose many people will disregard it. But is the defense of the liberties whose guarantees the Founding Fathers wrote into the Constitution a partisan issue? Not even McCarthy has explicitly said so, yet. I hope it never will become a partisan issue, for that would mean a schism in the nation as deep, and perhaps as irreparable, as we had in 1860. And then at

112

least there was principle on both sides; this time all the principle would be on one side, and it might not be the winning side, unless we stood up and fought for freedom.

The first and great commandment is, Don't let them scare you. For the men who are trying to do this to us are scared themselves. They are afraid that what they think will not stand critical examination; they are afraid that the principles on which this republic was founded and has been conducted are wrong. They will tell you that there is a hazard in the freedom of the mind, and of course there is, as in any freedom. In trying to think right you run the risk of thinking wrong. But there is no hazard at all, no uncertainty, in letting somebody else tell you what to think; that is sheer damnation. Judge Learned Hand, in that famous speech to the Board of Regents of the State of New York which has become practically the breviary of the friends of freedom, acknowledges the hazard and has the answer to it. "God knows there is a risk in refusing to act until the facts are all in; but is there not greater risk in abandoning the conditions of all rational inquiry? Risk for risk, for myself I had rather take my chance that some traitors will escape detection than spread abroad a spirit of general suspicion and distrust, which accepts rumor and gossip in place of undismayed and intimidated inquiry. . . .

113

The mutual conflict on which all else depends can be maintained only by an open mind and a brave reliance on free discussion. I do not say that these will suffice. Who knows but we are on a slope which leads down to aboriginal savagery? But of this I *am* sure—if we are to escape, we must not yield a foot upon demanding a fair field, and an honest race, to all ideas." This nation was conceived in liberty and dedicated to the principle—among others—that honest men may honestly disagree; that if they all say what they think, a majority of the people will be able to distinguish truth from error; that in the competition in the market place of ideas, the sounder ideas will in the long run win out. For almost four years past we have been engaged in a cold civil war—it is nothing less—testing whether any nation so conceived and so dedicated can long endure.

I believe it will endure, but only if we stand up for it. The frightened men who are trying to frighten us, because they have no faith in their country, are wrong; and even wronger are the smart men who are trying to use the frightened men for their own ends. The United States has worked; the principles of freedom on which it was founded—free thought as well as political liberty—have worked. This is the faith once delivered to the fathers—the faith for which they were willing to fight and, if necessary, die, but for

114

which they fought and won. Those men, whose heirs and beneficiaries we are, risked, and knew they were risking, their lives, their fortunes and their sacred honor. We shall have no heirs and beneficiaries, and shall deserve to have none, if we lack the courage to preserve the heritage they won for us. The national board of Americans for Democratic Action reminds us that this will remain the land of the free only so long as it is the home of the brave.

II

Improving on the Founding Fathers

IN THESE days when there is so much argument over what school children learn, if anything, it would be hazardous to say that every schoolboy knows—or indeed that any schoolboy knows—that William E. Gladstone once described our Constitution as the most wonderful work ever struck off at one time by the brain and purpose of man. And if some few schoolboys do know it, I wonder how many of them are aware that the author of this fulsome praise, when he was engaged in diplomatic negotiations with the United States, took a very dim view (as have other men before and since) of the constitutional requirement that treaties must be approved by two thirds of the Senate. Likewise many of our own citizens, who would regard criticism of the Constitution in general as no better than blasphemy, get greatly annoyed with anything in it that happens to interfere with something they want to do.

For all that it is a good Constitution—a Constitution that fits us; or perhaps, rather, after a hundred and sixty-four years, we have come to fit it. Yet good as it is, we have found it necessary to make twenty-two alterations in it. The first ten were virtually a part of the original document; of the rest, one merely canceled out another. Still there have been quite a number of changes, and people are trying to tinker with it still.

I do not say that some tinkering would not improve it; the provisions for the Presidential election could still let us in for trouble. The Electoral College is what somebody called it decades ago, a vermiform appendix; it has never in modern times become dangerously inflamed, but it has threatened once or twice, and it might be well to remove it by a simple operation before an emergency occurs. (We could, and I think we should, leave the electoral vote by states just as it is, even if the flesh-and-blood electors were abolished.) More trouble could come in the ambiguities remaining in the provisions for the Presidential succession. Some of them were clarified by statute in 1947; but we still do not know exactly what is the President's "inability to perform the powers and duties of his office," in which case the same shall devolve on the Vice-President. Normally that would mean that the President is too sick to do his job. Twice that

117

has occurred. The first time—in the simple world of 1881—there was not much to do; in 1919 there was plenty to do. But in neither case did his powers and duties devolve on the Vice-President, because neither the Constitution nor the statutes empowered anyone to determine when the inability began or (quite as important) when it ended. (In the case of President Garfield, of course, it ended when he died.) No one is so empowered now; if a President who had been disabled by illness thought he had got well, and a filling-in Vice-President—or a Vice-President backed by Congress—thought he had not, our government could be paralyzed. If a Vice-President did fill in, as none ever has, would he go back to being Vice-President again after the President recovered? Or would he, as some legal theorists have speculated, keep the job, with the former President as thoroughly out as if he had not recovered?

Congress could cure that and some other remaining ambiguities by legislation, though it has been repeatedly urged to do so in the past seventy-two years and has never done anything about it. It would take a constitutional amendment, however, to remove some other potentially disastrous possibilities. One of these is offered by the clause in the Constitution which provides that if no candidate has an electoral majority, the President shall be elected by the House of Representatives, with each state having one vote—the scanty population of Nevada counting for as much as a hundred times as many people in New York. Not since 1824 have we had to resort to that, but we always might have to—some men had high hopes of it in 1948; and if used again it would almost certainly mean, as it did the last time, the election of a minority candidate, as a result of such deals as are regarded with much less horror nowadays than they were in 1824. Moreover, the vote of each state is determined by the majority of the representatives in its delegation; it could easily happen that the party which had won the majority in the House by sweeping victories in the big states would not have won a majority of the state delegations, so we would get a President whom the House itself did not want.

This could be readily cured, though the cure would require amendment of the Constitution—simply provide that if the election were thrown into the House, each member should have one vote. Since this would be the House elected only two months before, as was not the case till recent years, it would be as fresh as possible an expression of the popular temper; and a President so elected could count on the support of Congress, in so far as any President ever can. But one other change would be needed, though this could be made by statute. If the House elects a President, it can't pick just anybody; it must choose from among the three candidates having the highest number of electoral votes. The possible trouble that this might give us was much in some people's minds early in December 1952, when General Eisenhower took his trip to Korea.

The Constitution provides that if the President-elect shall have died before the beginning of his term, the Vice-President-elect shall become President. But until the electoral vote has been cast in the several states on December 15—indeed until Congress formally counts it on January 6—there is neither a President-elect nor a Vice-President-elect—only a couple of citizens who have been recommended for those offices by an assembly of other citizens, a national party convention, which is unrecognized by the Constitution or the federal statutes. If a candidate dies before December 15—Eisenhower's trip to Korea ended on December 5—the party national committee, under its rules, could fill the vacancy on the ticket; there would no doubt be quite a dogfight among the supporters of various aspirants, but the impelling need of getting hold of the Presidency and its patronage would drive the committee to agree on a substitute and would lead all electors who could to vote for him.

But could they all? In twenty-seven states, including all the larger ones, the voting machine or ballot is not cluttered up with long lists of names of

120

individual electors; you voted for unnamed "electors for so-and-so." Of the 442 electors who voted for Eisenhower, 351 were chosen that way; only forty-eight of them—those from California and Massachusetts—were required by state law to vote for their party's nominee, whoever he might be, and only California is thoughtful enough to specify that he must still be alive. They couldn't vote for him if he was dead? Well, it has been done. The only Presidential candidate who ever died after the popular election, but before the electors met, was fortunately a defeated candidate—Horace Greeley in 1872. It didn't matter how his electors chose to scatter their complimentary votes, but three of them, even though they had been individually elected by name and were constitutionally entitled to a free choice, held that they had been elected to vote for Horace Greeley and nobody else; and they did vote for him, though he was in his grave. (They might not have done so, of course, if the election had been so close that their three votes would have decided it.)

Votes for a dead man don't count, according to the decision of a Massachusetts court in a local election, and other courts would no doubt hold the same view; probably, in so far as a layman can guess, electors chosen to vote for a dead man would be permitted to vote instead for the party committee's substitute—if the original candidate had died before December 15.

But if he died between that date and January 6, when the vote was counted, it would be found that the majority of votes had been cast for a dead man and were consequently null and void. In that case would the Vice-President-elect automatically become President? Not at all; he could succeed only a President-elect who had died, and there would be none. The House of Representatives would have to choose from among the three candidates with the highest number of electoral votes, and ordinarily only two candidates have any. If the man with the higher number were dead, the House would have to elect the man who had lost the popular election in November. An honorable man wouldn't accept it under such conditions? Well, he would be under terrific pressure to accept it. His party would argue that a man who had made a good showing against a successful Presidential candidate could certainly have licked the Vice-President if he had been at the head of the ticket (assuming that he was of the quality of most of our Vice-Presidents); some candidates would be unable to resist the temptation. The Twentieth Amendment declares that Congress may provide by law for the case of the death of any of the persons from whom the House of Representatives may choose a President, but Congress has never got around to it. It had better, lest someday it might have to be done in a hurry, after the unexpected death of a victorious candi-

122

date; when the pull of partisan and personal ambitions might make it impossible to get anything done in time.

And Congress had better give some thought to defining Presidential disability—what it is, who decides when it begins and who decides when it has ended. This is not at all an easy question, but it should be studied and settled when there is no argument currently on foot; otherwise it might come up again, and prove impossible to solve, in a period of even more bitter partisan hatred, and in an even shakier international situation, than that of 1919.

One other constitutional amendment is badly needed in the atomic age—provisions such as have repeatedly been proposed in the last seven years, but never seriously discussed, to take care of the unlikely but not impossible contingency that a bomb might wipe out a majority of Congress or all persons in the statutory line of Presidential succession. These last could be scattered in case of a threatened air raid, but Congress cannot scatter if it is to legislate. Vacant Senate seats can be temporarily filled by appointment, but there would be no way to replace a suddenly deceased majority of the House.

But even if our Constitution has these loopholes in it, it is a pretty good Constitution none the less. It does not establish a very efficient government, but it

123

was not intended to. As Mr. Justice Brandeis once said, "The doctrine of the separation of powers was adopted, not to promote efficiency but to preclude the exercise of arbitrary power. The purpose was not to avoid friction, but by means of the inevitable friction to save the people from autocracy." The government of England, in which an executive with a large majority in the House of Commons can do pretty nearly anything it wants to do, works well for the English, who are a calm and equable nation; if we had such a system we might tear ourselves to pieces.

But if our government was deliberately made not very efficient, it has always proved efficient enough to do what it had to do, even though President Lincoln had to subject the Constitution to some interpretations which must have rattled the bones of the Founding Fathers. This was not the idea, at first. The men who had won the Revolutionary War seem to have thought, for a brief period, that they could get along with the Articles of Confederation—a government which was about as near no government as any civilized nation ever tried to operate. "The decentralizing democrats," says Herbert Agar, "had written the constitution they wanted, and it was a good constitution for their purposes; but their purposes were not adequate in a world of power and cruelty and greed."

124

Yes, but it was not only the decentralizing demo-crats. I suspect that one strong reason why con-servatives as well as liberals accepted the Articles of Confederation without much argument was the same emotion that displayed itself in 1919 and in 1945—the feeling of a nation which has just won a great war that now it has won all its wars, solved all its prob-lems, and can live happily ever after. "Nothing would have pleased them better," writes Howard Swiggett, "than to have the loose Confederation suffice for a government, Europe to leave them alone, and they to till the soil and make the rivers navigable to the Western Waters"—though Washington's famous let-ter to Lafayette, which he quotes in that connection, could conceivably have been inspired by the optimism of a real-estate developer as well as by (undoubtedly its principal motive) the vision of a patriot.

This was an ancient dream. Most of these men (though not Washington) had had a classical educa-tion; they may have been thinking in terms of Hor-ace's Sixteenth Epode—a nation tearing itself away from the endless wars and turmoil of Europe to find itself a new home in the Happy Land beyond the seas, where there are never any bad crop years, or cloud-bursts, nor even any snakes. This was not a precisely accurate picture of the eastern United States in 1781; but there were always "the fertile plains of the Ohio," where, as Washington wrote, "anyone who is heavy laden may repair hither and abound, as in the Land of Promise with milk and honey." And there was Horace's climactic promise, which seemed to have been fulfilled—*"Iuppiter illa piae secrevit littora genti."*

Even on this favored continent such sentiments were not universal. They were not shared, for instance, by the United Empire Loyalists, chopping new homes for themselves out of the Canadian wilderness; in their eyes, the nation that had chased them out was hardly a *gens pia*. And it did not take long to prove that the Articles of Confederation were based on a much too optimistic view of human nature, both abroad and at home; they had not only failed to abolish original sin, but had not much constricted its operations. All credit to our ancestors (or most of them) for seeing very soon that the Articles would not do (and perhaps almost as much credit for not doing anything about it till the Congress under the Confederation had accomplished its one great act of statesmanship, the ordinance for the government of the Northwest Territory). When the Constitutional Convention met, its members were zealous to take precautions against executive, and still more against legislative, tyranny; but they knew that for all their precautions they must still make a government that would work.

126

In these times perhaps more than ever, except in the crisis of civil war, we need a government that can do what it has to do. It may be that, as optimists hope, the leaders of world Communism may someday abate their zeal and give up their hopes of world conquest—settle down to a more or less peaceful coexistence, as did Islam with Christendom (though only after a thousand years, and only when the military superiority of Christendom had been definitely established). But till that happy day comes we shall need a government that can do what has to be done.

It would seem that such a situation calls for as high a degree of national unity as is possible in a democracy, short of a shooting war. Instead of which, as I was saying earlier, we have a good many citizens who seem to think that the enemy is their fellow citizens who disagree with them, rather than somebody abroad; and many others—some of them eminent, more of them rich—think that the enemy is not the government of the Soviet Union or of the Chinese People's Republic, but the government of the United States. During the Roosevelt and Truman administrations it could be supposed that their enemy was only a liberal government; but since January of 1953 it has been evident that their enemy is no particular administration but government itself, and they are continually trying to weaken its power—not only by

127

less forthright methods but by the frontal attack of constitutional amendment.

The only one of these endeavors that has so far succeeded is probably the one that will do least harm, but it could do some harm at that; indeed it has done some harm already by imbedding its underlying assumptions in the structure of our government. The Eightieth Congress proposed, and a sufficient number of state legislatures ratified, the Twenty-second Amendment to the Constitution, limiting any man's tenure of the Presidential office hereafter to two terms. The question of Presidential re-eligibility (once or oftener) had been thoroughly debated in the Constitutional Convention, by men possibly as able and patriotic as the members of the Eightieth Congress; and they chose to impose no limit. The argument against limitation was classically stated by Alexander Hamilton in the *Federalist*. There are times when a nation absolutely needs a particular man in a particular situation; don't call him indispensable if you don't want to, but there are crises—the outbreak of war, for instance—when it would be foolish to substitute inexperience for experience. There is a further argument that would not have appealed much to Hamilton but that has some pertinence in contemporary American political theory; to say that you can't select what Washington once called the man most capable of serv-

128

ing the public in some great emergency means that you don't trust the people. If in some crisis now beyond foreseeing they should feel that they need a particular man, the wisdom of the Eightieth Congress has decreed that they can't have him if he has served two terms already.

I heard the entire debate in the House of Representatives on the resolution proposing this amendment. No attempt was made to refute Hamilton's argument (I doubt if many members had ever heard of it); indeed until the last two minutes of a long afternoon there was no reasoned attempt to support the change at all. Then Mr. Michener of Michigan came up with an argument that would have been pertinent if true—that a President long in office could fill up the public service, in low positions as well as high, with his appointees, who would always vote for him in order to keep their jobs. Unfortunately for this thesis the heaviest concentration of federal employees in any area where they can vote is in the suburban counties around Washington in Maryland and Virginia; and during the Roosevelt and Truman administrations those counties had the habit of going Republican. Many of their inhabitants have since been fired; if those who have not been fired have a proper gratitude to the administration that spared them, while a thousand fell at their side and ten thou-

129

sand at their right hand, they may provide belated support for Mr. Michener's argument.

But all the rest of that House debate was one long hymn of hate against Roosevelt; men who couldn't lick him when he was living relieved their feelings by dancing on his grave. The psychiatric value of such an emotional release was no doubt considerable; but it might have been accomplished with less injury to the nation by the process which the Roman Senate, after the death of an Emperor whom they hadn't liked, used to call *damnatio memoriae*—repealing his enactments, smashing his statues and chiseling his name off the public buildings erected during his administration.

That Congress, particularly the Senate, distrusts any President is an old story; it began when President Washington had been in office only three months. That Congress distrusts the Supreme Court, unless it happens to agree with the Congressional majority, also is not news. What I had never expected to see, till it happened, was the Senate distrusting the Senate. Yet that is the meaning of the famous Bricker amendment, in whose introduction Mr. Bricker persuaded no less than sixty-three of his colleagues to join him, limiting the treaty-making power. Mr. Bricker proposed it in an impassioned speech in which he painted a horrendous picture of a revolutionary President, supported by corrupt senators, putting over a treaty that would sell the United States down the river into God knows what abyss of tyranny and atheism. This argument had been anticipated by John Jay in the *Federalist;* a man must have been very unfortunate in his intercourse with the world, he said, or possess a heart very susceptible of such impressions, who would believe that the President and two thirds of the Senate would ever be capable of such unworthy conduct. But it must be admitted that this was written before our present form of government was in operation. John Jay had not yet known any senators; John Bricker has known a lot of them. He knows more of them than I do, and knows them better; it is not for me to question his estimate of his colleagues.

The Bricker amendment is of course aimed at that clause in Article VI of the Constitution which provides that laws made in pursuance of the Constitution, and all treaties made under the authority of the United States, shall be the supreme law of the land, anything in the Constitution or the laws of any of the states notwithstanding. From what is this "authority of the United States" derived? Obviously from the Constitution itself; the Tenth Amendment spells it out that that is all the authority the federal govern-

131

ment has got. So the clause of the Bricker amendment, in its latest and much modified form, declaring that a provision of a treaty which conflicts with the Constitution shall be of no force and effect, merely insists that the Constitution means what it says. (To quiet the fears of the timorous, must we thereafter have still another amendment declaring that the Bricker amendment means what it says?)

The difference in language, in this reference to laws and to treaties, was apparently put in to validate such treaties as had been made under the Articles of Confederation, including the treaty with England that recognized our independence. (Under the Bricker amendment, which provides that a treaty shall become effective as internal law only through legislation which would be valid in the absence of a treaty, would Congress have to pass a law declaring that the United States is free and independent?) Supporters of the amendment make much of the language used by Mr. Justice Holmes in *Missouri v. Holland,* thirty-three years ago, that "it is open to question whether 'the authority of the United States' means more than the formal acts prescribed to make the convention"; they conveniently ignore the fact that his next words were "we do not mean to imply that there are no qualifications to the treaty-making power, but they must be ascertained in a different way"; and later

132

that "the treaty in question does not contravene any prohibitory words to be found in the Constitution; the only question is whether it is forbidden by some invisible radiation from the general terms of the Tenth Amendment." They also ignore the fact that the courts have repeatedly held that no treaty can deprive a citizen of the rights guaranteed by the Constitution. All they have to stand on, legally, is a single sentence in *Missouri v. Holland*, counteracted if not contradicted by the following sentence, and a single decision by a lower court in California, which was overruled by the state supreme court.

It cannot be denied, however, that the Bricker amendment has received formidable legal support. Mr. John Foster Dulles, when he was in private life, made a powerful argument in its favor; when he became Secretary of State he made an equally powerful argument against it, performing this difficult somersault with an agility that ought to qualify him for a job under the Big Top. The American Bar Association endorsed the amendment a couple of years ago; in the summer of 1953 Judge John J. Parker vigorously urged its House of Delegates to rescind that action, but they refused—though one member of the House thought the principal argument for the refusal was that the American Bar Association would lose caste by changing its mind.

133

That the Bricker amendment, even in its modified version, would hobble if not cripple the treaty-making power is evident; that is what it is for. It does not go quite so far as a proposal advanced during the argument over the adoption of the Constitution, that treaties—all treaties, whether or not they involved any internal rearrangements—should be repealable by act of Congress. John Jay had something to say about that too: "A treaty is only another name for a bargain, and it would be impossible to find a nation who would make any bargain with us which should be binding on them absolutely, but on us only so long and so far as we may think proper to be bound by it." And there might be almost as much reluctance to make a treaty which, after two thirds of the Senate had approved it, would still be no good until both Houses of Congress had given further approval by passing a law.

Of course some treaties fall into that class already—those whose execution requires an appropriation. As early as 1796 the House of Representatives had fought for and established its right to act on appropriations, even if a treaty clearly called for them. And the Constitutional Convention had considered, and rejected, an alternative method for approving treaties—by a majority of both Houses of Congress. The provision that two thirds of the Senate must approve was adopted instead to guarantee that neither Northern nor Southern states could put over a treaty disastrous to the interests of the other section; we might have had no Constitution without it. If it was a mistake, it was a mistake unavoidable at the time; the Founding Fathers did not foresee the rise of parties, but it is hard to see how they could have done any better with the immediate problem they had to deal with.

But the two-thirds rule has made so much trouble that there has been increasing support in recent years for the other method—approval by a majority in both Houses. That support, naturally, has been most evident in that body which furiously insists that it is not the lower House of Congress but a legislative organ coeval and coequal with the Senate. But the makers of the Constitution had other objections to that, besides the decisive one of the conflict of sectional interests. Those objections were summed up by Hamilton in the *Federalist;* the "fluctuating and multitudinous" composition of the House would make it unsuitable for such responsibility. This has less force now that the Senate is fifty per cent more multitudinous than was the House in 1789, but the argument that we should change that provision of the Constitution is only sounding brass and tinkling cymbal; a change would require the consent of two thirds of the Senate,

135

which would never give up such a cherished prerogative.

Yet this method has often been employed in substance 'if not in name; the executive agreement supported by joint resolution, which calls only for a majority in each House, has proved in recent years an immensely useful, perhaps an indispensable, instrument for getting things done, even if one third plus one of the senators do not want them done. (And not merely in recent years; Texas and Hawaii were both annexed by that method.) So useful that the earlier Hoover Commission's task force on foreign affairs—two very able former Assistant Secretaries of State, Harvey Bundy and James Grafton Rogers—recommended that while "treaties may still be advisable in certain instances," they should be replaced as far as possible by this other expedient.

And is this not what Bricker proposes? Not at all; he would still have treaties approved by two thirds of the Senate and then, if they involve anything that could be called internal legislation, by a law passed by a majority of both Houses besides. Few foreign governments would be eager to jump that double hurdle, not to speak of the famous "which clause"— legislation "which would be valid in the absence of a treaty." More of that in a moment. But there are all kinds of other executive agreements—some made

136

under the President's constitutional powers as commander in chief, others as incidental to the conduct of foreign affairs—which do not have Congressional validation but which could be regulated by Congress under the Bricker amendment. When you speak of such executive agreements the frightened men think of Yalta, which has become a four-letter word—though when the Senate Foreign Relations Committee actually looked at the Yalta agreement recently they found it was nowhere near so bad as propaganda represented it. Anyway, I doubt if the territorial and political arrangements made at Yalta, even if the Russians had lived up to their promises, would have been valid unless approved by the Senate like any other treaty.

But there are literally thousands of other executive agreements—military, political and economic—without which, as both the Secretary and the Undersecretary of State told the Senate last year, the day-to-day business of conducting our foreign relations could not be carried on. Especially now that we have allies, and troops stationed abroad in friendly countries. Congress could not possibly foresee all the occasions on which such agreements might be needed, nor regulate them in such a way as to take care of every contingency, even if it approached them in a friendly mood; and the attitude of the supporters of the Brick-

137

er amendment seems to make sure that the mood would be one of suspicion if not of hostility. This provision would practically handcuff not only the State Department but the military establishment— that is, the President as commander in chief—in dealing with foreign powers.

But to many citizens all these arguments are outweighed by fear. Ostensibly the fear that motivates them is fear of the United Nations, but their real motive is fear of the government of the United States. As a New York *Times* editorial put it, it is "fear of ourselves, of our traditional processes of government, and of the ability of our properly constituted representatives to look after our own interests. It represents an effort to erect a sort of voodoo wall of rigid constitutional and statutory safeguards to protect us from the realities of political life."

For documentation of that you can read the speeches of my old college friend Frank Holman, past president of the American Bar Association, who seems to have played Svengali to Bricker's Trilby in this whole affair and whose vision of the future is even more hagridden than Bricker's. "Who can say that such precious rights as jury trial and the writ of habeas corpus may not, in the opinion of the Supreme Court, have to yield to the common denominator of basic rights as understood by fifty-seven other nations?" (Arthur H. Dean writes in *Foreign Affairs* that the Supreme Court is about as likely to do that as to reverse its decision in *Marbury v. Madison* and deprive itself of the right to nullify laws that conflict with the Constitution.) But Holman sees another frightful prospect; a treaty might "accord to the nationals of all countries the privilege to aspire to the office of President of the United States." So, if we don't adopt the Bricker amendment, we are likely to get a Russian or a Chinese President—and not Chiang Kai-shek, who is apparently the favorite candidate of some of our statesmen. Holman did stop short of the ultimate absurdities offered as serious arguments by some people on his side—that the Genocide Convention, which there is little chance that the United States will ever adopt, would permit foreigners (Russians, no doubt) to invade this country to punish lynching, and would forbid the practice of contraception, now illegal only in Connecticut.

Well, when people say they see flying saucers it is not much use telling them that it is only an optical illusion; let's see if there is anything we can hold onto. On the Bricker-Holman theory we can't trust the President, or the Senate, or the Supreme Court (or even the House of Representatives, much); where then is our hope? Ah, here is where the famous "which clause" comes in. "A treaty shall become effective as internal law only through legislation which would be valid in absence of a treaty." This is the one which knocks out the constitutional provision that treaties made under the authority of the United States shall be the supreme law of the land, "anything in the constitution or the laws of any state to the contrary notwithstanding." The United States as a sovereign power could not make arrangements in dealing with other powers unless they covered matters ordinarily within Congressional authority. That is to say, if that very able lawyer the Secretary of State has correctly analyzed this proposal (on his second try), many treaties would require the approval of all forty-eight states to become effective.

That this would cause a certain reluctance on the part of foreign powers to enter into treaties with us is obvious; but the main point about it is that here at last we discover the only officials whom these scared bunnies supporting the Bricker amendment really trust—the members of the state legislatures, the very men whom the Founding Fathers distrusted above all others.

If we feel that way we had better repeal the whole Constitution and go back to the Articles of Confederation, with no executive, no judiciary, no taxing power in Congress, and no state compelled to do anything it didn't want to do. And we face just that possibility, though I do not expect that it will be realized, in another proposal for amendment.

The Constitution provides an alternative process of amendment which has never been used—application to Congress by the legislatures of two thirds of the states to call a convention for the proposing of amendments, which thereafter would not have to run the gantlet of Congress but would become part of the Constitution when ratified by three fourths of the states. Congress on such application must call the convention; nobody knows how its members would be chosen, whether by popular vote or by state legislatures (or even by appointment, since Congress could apparently enact any method that it might prefer). Application has been made by some twenty-odd legislatures, not far short of the necessary two thirds, in the interest of one particular amendment. But the Constitution says that the purpose of this convention shall be the proposing of amendments, plural; many eminent lawyers hold that it could propose as many as it wanted to—could, if it wished, propose to throw the entire Constitution aside. It wouldn't do that, of course; but I am sure that if such a convention ever met, there would be some very determined attacks on the Bill of Rights—the Fifth Amendment particularly, and very likely the First one too.

These attacks might or might not succeed; the

141

amendment most likely to be approved by such a convention would be the one in whose interest it was proposed—that Congress be forbidden to impose income and estate taxes above twenty-five per cent, except in case of a major war. In this form it was too raw to gain much support, as soon as people began talking about it, so it was materially modified by Senator Dirksen and Representative Chauncey Reed; but no matter how thin you slice it, it tastes the same. It is a program for transferring as much as possible of the tax burden from the rich to the poor—about sixteen billion dollars, according to an estimate by the New Council for American Business. I have read elaborate arguments that it is nothing of the sort, which are not at all convincing. In these times, and in such times as we are likely to have to live through for several decades, the government will need a great deal of money; it is going to have to get it out of somebody, painful as this will be to all of us. And the argument that the twenty-five-per-cent limit would give relief to the lower brackets is not impressive; it could mean that people who now pay twenty-two per cent would have to pay twenty-five. Or else—and this of course is what the twenty-five-per-centers are shooting at—a sales tax, which would fall most heavily on the people who have to spend their incomes, with no surplus for investment.

142

Ironically, it looks at this writing as if these gentlemen might get their sales tax, if it can be jammed through Congress; but they will still be stuck with their income tax too. For the government still needs money, and the idea of reducing that need by disarming our defenses does not seem to have taken hold very widely, especially in the Northern cities exposed to enemy attack.

This twenty-five-per-cent proposal, however, is not the only competitor for the honor of being the Twenty-third Amendment. There is another—that the government be forbidden to engage in any kind of business whatsoever. Probably most of the men behind this have their eyes on atomic-energy and public-power developments—which they may get their hooks on anyway, under present policies—but they have singularly neglected their best talking point: that if this amendment were adopted, the government would have to sell the Post Office Department to private industry.

There would be no bidders on this insolvent institution unless all lids on the rates were taken off. With rates boosted to a point that would show a profit, the flood of publicity and promotional material that now overloads the desk of everybody in the news business would shrink to the vanishing point; and if first-class mail cost a quarter instead of three cents, fewer letters would be written, and fewer people would get

143

into trouble. Also it is possible that private industry might be able to solve the problem of putting gum on our postage stamps that would stick, which seems to be beyond the capacity of Postmaster General Summerfield, as it was of his Democratic predecessors.

A more modest amendment, proposed by Senator McCarran, went through the Senate in the spring of 1953 without difficulty, as might have been expected, but died in the House, as might also have been expected. It simply provided that the President could not take possession of private property except in a manner prescribed by act of Congress. The general public may have supposed that the Supreme Court had said just that, in dealing with the President's seizure of the steel mills in 1952; but the eagle eye of McCarran saw deeper. What the Supreme Court said was that the President could not do it *in those circumstances;* it did not say that he could never do it in any circumstances. Even some of those who concurred in the opinion that slapped him down suggested that in time of insurrection or invasion (and a general atomic-bombing attack might be as serious as invasion) he might have more authority.

"In the absence of action by Congress," said Mr. Justice Clark, "the President's independent power to act depends on the gravity of the situation confronting the nation." The McCarran amendment clearly

144

calls for action by Congress; but can Congress predict, and provide against, every emergency in which quick action might be essential? What the McCarran amendment means is that no unforeseen contingency shall ever occur; and I doubt if to guarantee that is within the power of Congress, even if the Constitution should grant it such authority.

All these proposed amendments—as well as the Twenty-second which was actually adopted—have one thing in common: they would weaken a government which their proponents evidently regard as too strong. Fear of a too strong federal government is nothing new; it was widely and eloquently expressed in the debate over the adoption of the Constitution. There is, however, one difference: in 1788 those who feared a strong government were mostly the poor and the champions of the poor; now it is the champions of the rich—who are richer and more powerful than could have been foreseen when this government was established and who, if the government were weakened, would be more powerful still.

Whether this country would be better off, in a time of placid international relations, if the rich were more powerful than they have been in the twenty years before January 1953 is a legitimately debatable question. But those were not years—at least the last dozen—of placid international relations; nor will the next twenty years be so either. In this "business-man's administration" the rich will certainly be more influential than they have been in the twenty years preceding it, but it looks as if they may avoid the grosser errors of the period from 1921 to 1933; and in any case the structure of government still stands, with little damage, and is in the hands of men who seem to realize that the international situation is and will continue to be of overriding importance. We should buy an increase in the power of any class in the community at too high a price if it meant weakening the government of the United States in a time when it may have to be able to act firmly, and to act fast.

III

News and the Whole Truth

EACH spring the members of the American Newspaper Publishers Association assemble in convention and spend a good deal of their time eulogizing themselves. Conventions of editors and reporters, whether for newspapers or radio news, are more practical and less complacent. The American news business, press and radio, certainly deserves some eulogies; it is the most copious in the world, and I think its average quality is at least as good as any other's. But it is not yet good enough. Too often we tell the customers not what is really going on, but what seems to be going on. And I am not referring to the small minority of newspapers, and the smaller minority of newspapermen, who don't want to tell the truth, but to the great majority who do want to tell the truth but often fall short.

Too much of our news is one-dimensional, when truth has three dimensions (or maybe more); we still have inadequate defenses against men who try to load the news with propaganda; and in some fields the vast and increasing complexity of the news makes it continually more difficult—especially for us Washington reporters—to tell the public what really happened. Some of these failings are due to encrusted habits of the news business, which can be changed only slowly, but which many men are now trying to change; some of them will be harder to cure because they are only the reverse side of some of our greatest merits, and it is difficult to see how to get rid of them without endangering the merits too.

The merits which entail the worst drawbacks are competition and the striving for objectivity, and we should be much worse off without either. But objectivity often leans over backward so far that it makes the news business merely a transmission belt for pretentious phonies. As for competition, there is no doubt that the nation is much better served by three wire services—the Associated Press, the United Press and the International News Service, sometimes supplemented by the English Reuters—and by several radio networks than it would be by monopoly in either field. But competition means an overemphasis on speed, as has been noted by the Associated Press Managing Editors (not the editors of the AP but the men who use its service); and sometimes it leads to an exaggerated build-up.

148

Like most radio newsmen, I am heavily dependent on the wire services. I am supposed to be aware of all the world's news and to report what seems to me most important or that to which I can add something in the way of interpretation. But I can't cover it all myself—not even all that happens in Washington; usually I cover about one story a day on foot, get angles or elucidations on half a dozen others by telephone, and must depend on the wire services for the rest. Experience has taught me, when the versions of the same story given by two wire services differ materially, to prefer the less exciting; the other might have been souped up to beat the competition.

President Truman announced his decision not to run again at the end of his speech at the Jefferson-Jackson Day dinner on March 29, 1952—an extemporaneous addition to a script distributed several hours in advance. All the wire services sent out the text, of course; early editions of the Sunday papers were going to press and had to have it at the earliest moment. The UP and INS merely sent out the text; the AP, desirous of making everything clear (and maybe of getting the jump on the competition), prefaced it with a lead saying that the President made no disclosure of his intentions. Papers carrying that lead were on the street as he was disclosing his intentions. At least one radio station—a good one, too—

149

writing its eleven-o'clock news out of the AP, went on the air and said that he had made no disclosure of his intentions; whereas many of the listeners a few minutes earlier had heard the President say he wouldn't run.

I do not suppose that any of the wire services ever consciously sacrifices accuracy to speed; but speed is what counts most, because what every wire service wants is to get newspapers to use its story rather than its competitors' stories. I have seen many service messages on press-association wires boasting about how many minutes, or even how many seconds, they were ahead of the competition, how their story got the play. I have seldom if ever seen a message saying, "While our story was unfortunately a few minutes behind time, it had more truth in it." Yet these outfits live, and must live, by competition; and we are better off with that competition, whatever its shortcomings, than we should be without it. One of the wire services has a motto, "Get it there first—but first get it right." I am sure they all try to do that; I am not sure that a wire service which actually succeeded in doing it would last long against the competition.

Nine days before the Germans surrendered in 1945 there was a great, though brief, flurry over an AP report from San Francisco—where the constituent assembly of the United Nations was then meeting—that they had surrendered and an announcement could be expected at any moment. The story was sent by one of the ablest reporters in the country; he got it from a person described as a high American official, who wouldn't let his name be used—something that happens every day; and it may have been mass self-delusion that persuaded many people that the high official was the Secretary of State, who would have known. Actually it was Senator Connally; but he might have known too; and if the reporter had stopped to check up with the Secretary of State or anybody else, the competition might have got the story out ahead of him. So it was left to the President of the United States to do the checking up and find out that the story was false.

That time, the AP got a beat on a surrender that didn't happen; nine days later it got a beat on the one that did happen—because one of its correspondents broke a release date that fifteen other correspondents observed. Now some of those hold-for-release regulations of the SHAEF public-relations officers—imposed in an endeavor to get simultaneous release in all Allied capitals—may have seemed ridiculous; the German radio was already announcing the surrender. Nevertheless the sixteen correspondents who had covered the actual ceremony had all promised to

151

hold the story till a certain hour. Fifteen of them did; one of them did not. If that incident had been repeated once or twice it would have made it extremely difficult for any correspondent to get any news.

Here the fault clearly lay with the pressure of competition. I am told, by a man who should know, that the three principal AP correspondents on the Western front had identical instructions; besides competing with everybody else they were competing with one another, presumably on the theory that that would keep them on their toes. It is not surprising that one of them got so far up on his toes that he fell over on his face.

It was the United Press that ended the old war four days early in 1918—an incident now remembered chiefly because Roy Howard, who was responsible for what was then the greatest boner in American news history, was able enough to live it down. He happened to be in a position to see, quite legitimately, what appeared to be an official dispatch; and he flashed it without checking up on it. It was in contradiction to the known intention of ending the war four days later; but I do not suppose there was or is a reporter for any wire service, American or foreign, who would not have done what Roy Howard did. It is hard to say how much actual harm was done, aside from taking the edge off the celebration of the real armistice; but there is some reason to believe that the message that fooled Howard was planted by a German agent in Paris, who presumably hoped that it would do harm.

Now these were not bad reporters; they were all good reporters, among the best; but they were all in too big a hurry, for fear somebody else would beat them to it. We have seen many forecasts of what will happen in the next war, if we have one. I do not know what the course of operations will be; the one thing I feel safe in predicting is that some American reporter will end it a few days before it actually ends, and the families of men who were killed after he said it was over will, for the rest of their lives, be convinced that you can't believe what you see in the papers.

Most Russian propaganda nowadays needs no fumigation in this country; it defeats itself. The Russians appear to regard us as enemies, and their routine propaganda is put out with no expectation that it will have any effect on us but may only help to keep other nations as neutral as possible as long as possible. There is one outstanding exception—the occasional answers that Stalin used to vouchsafe to inquiries from American correspondents.

Certainly an "interview" with Stalin would have

been a great journalistic achievement. But the many reporters who tried it never interviewed Stalin, asking him questions face to face. They had to send in their questions through diplomatic channels; and Stalin answered them or not, according to whether the answers would do some good to Stalin. The kind of questions he would answer were the kind asked him by Kingsbury Smith of the INS in January 1949 and by James Reston of the New York *Times* in December 1952. To Smith he said that Russia would join the United States in a declaration that we had no intention of going to war with each other (a promise which, in somewhat different form, was a staple of Russian propaganda—and Russia had made such promises to other nations and broken them); that Russia would join us in gradual disarmament to that end (the Russians always say they are for disarmament, on their terms); that Stalin had no objection to meeting President Truman—a meeting which the President was known to regard as useless; and that Russia would lift the Berlin blockade if the Western powers would postpone the establishment of a West German state— prevention of such establishment being the obvious purpose of the Berlin blockade. The blockade was lifted some months later, and endeavors have been made to represent Smith's questions as at least partly responsible—which seems open to doubt in view of the fact that the Allies had gone ahead and set up the West German state before the blockade was lifted.

To Reston, Stalin said that he believed Russia and the United States could live together peacefully (if he had said they couldn't, that *would* have been news); that the source of the present trouble in the world was the cold war against the Soviet Union (all our fault, none of it his); that he would like to meet President Eisenhower to help ease world tensions; and finally that he would co-operate in a new diplomatic approach to end the Korean war. And indeed some months later the Korean war was ended; but the diplomatic approach that led up to that result was begun only after Stalin was dead.

From both these sets of answers you got the picture of good old benevolent Uncle Joe, who wanted to live in peace with everybody; and you got vast publicity for certain propaganda arguments that Stalin wanted to get before the world. He could have got them before the world by a statement in *Pravda,* but that would have attracted far less attention than answers to well-known American reporters. Most editorials analyzed the Stalin statements for what they were; but their analyses were read by far fewer people than saw the news stories on the front page.

Now Smith and Reston, while of course they wanted answers from Stalin, did not want these particular answers; indeed these were not the questions they wanted to ask him. Each man had sent him several previous sets of questions which he ignored. Like a smart batter facing a pitcher who is trying to cut the corners of the plate, he refused to reach for the wide ones and finally made them lay it in the groove. It is an effective technique; Malenkov has not yet tried it, at this writing, but he probably will if he lasts long enough.

Reporting of the Korean war was in general very good—some of it, such as Homer Bigart's dispatches in the early months to the New York *Herald Tribune*, exceedingly good; but we let the enemy slip a few fast ones past us. There were two English-speaking Communist correspondents, the Englishman Alan Winnington and the Australian Wilfred Burchett, who had been with the Communist armies and then came down to Panmunjom to cover the truce talks. British and Australian correspondents would have nothing to do with them; but some of the Americans were innocent enough to suppose, at first, that they were just newspapermen like themselves, and quoted them as authorities not only for conditions behind the enemy lines but for what was going on in the truce-talk tents. I am told by correspondents returned from Korea that sometimes they had to use what they got from Winnington and Burchett because they could get nothing out of our public-information officers. But what did they get out of Winnington and Burchett? Not objective truth, you may be sure, unless by accident.

Enemy propaganda in Korea also made hay with photographs—many of them taken by an American, Frank Noel, an AP photographer who was a prisoner; but transmitted to our side of the lines, of course, by the Communists. According to those photographs the life of a prisoner of war in North Korea was indeed a happy one. We saw groups of prisoners, warmly dressed against the Korean winter—fat, well fed and smiling. Well—a man who knows that his picture is going to be printed in the American papers where his family will see it wants to look cheerful; they feel bad enough about his being a prisoner and would feel worse if they thought he was mistreated.

There were plenty of American prisoners who were not well fed and warmly dressed, but Noel was not allowed to take their pictures; his guides hurried him right past them till they found somebody whose picture, when passed on for publication in the American press, would be good propaganda for the Communists. In the circumstances it is no wonder they allowed a camera for Noel to be sent in through the lines; and some doubt remains as to whether this display of journalistic enterprise really served a useful purpose. These pictures were the truth, of what they depicted; but they certainly were very far from the whole truth about the prison camps in North Korea.

The United Nations Commission on Freedom of Information has been trying to work out an international code of ethics for newsmen—not an easy task in view of the different concepts of news (and of ethics) on the two sides of the Iron Curtain. The first and I believe the only one so far adopted (by a vote of six to nothing with five abstaining) says only that reporters, editors and commentators shall do their best to make sure that the information the public receives is factually accurate, with no fact willfully distorted and no essential fact deliberately suppressed.

I don't know why the American delegate abstained from voting for that innocuous declaration, unless for the reason that it doesn't go far enough. What is factual accuracy? Not merely what a man says, for sometimes he has said the contradictory thing in times past; and sometimes, indeed, what he says is known to be false. Truth has three dimensions; but the practices of the American news business—practices adopted in a praiseworthy ambition to be objective—too often give us only one-dimensional news—factually accurate so far as it goes, but very far indeed from the whole truth.

There was not much objectivity in the American

press through most of the nineteenth century; if a story touched on the political or economic interest of the editor or owner, it was usually written so as to make his side look good. Some papers still follow that practice; but most of them, for some decades past, have accepted the principle that they ought to try to be objective in the news columns, leaving argument to the editorial page. Publish everything that is said on both sides of a controversial issue and let the reader make up his mind. A noble theory; but suppose that men who talk on one side (or on both) are known to be lying to serve their own personal interest; or suppose they don't know what they are talking about. To call attention to these facts, except on the editorial page, would not, according to most newspaper practice, be objective. Yet in the complex news of today how many readers have enough personal knowledge to distinguish fact from fiction, ignorance from knowledge, interest from impartiality?

This practice is perhaps not quite so prevalent now as it was twenty-five years or so ago—in the golden age of Calvin Coolidge, when it was the general opinion that things are what they seem. In those days, if the Honorable John P. Hoozis was an important person, you were likely to see him quoted at length in the newspapers on almost any subject, with no indication that he knew nothing at all about it, or no indication that he had a strong personal interest in getting people to believe what he said—even if the editor who printed the story happened to know it. He was an important man; he had made a statement; and it would not have been objective not to print it. We have been getting away from that dead-pan objectivity of late years—or were, till the rise of Senator McCarthy.

He may be a unique case, but he is far from the only case in which the press (and radio) misinforms the nation through the habit of regarding anything that the Honorable John P. Hoozis says as news. Take an example more to the point, since there seems no question of any deliberate intention to mislead. In 1951 Pat Hurley was testifying in the MacArthur hearings—former Major General, former Secretary of War, former Ambassador to China Pat Hurley. About military affairs and Chinese politics he might have been supposed to know something—though even that may be open to doubt in view of his remark, some years ago, that Chinese Communists are just like Oklahoma Republicans except that they carry guns. Somehow he had got off the subject and into criticism of some hearings by Congressional committees, which had acquitted people whom he considered guilty.

"For instance," he said, "the hearings on the atomic energy organization. I read the report of the committee that heard that case, and it was a clean bill of

160

health, a certificate of purity and patriotism for everybody in the organization. Yet less than six months,
just a little after, Dr. Klaus Fuchs confessed in London; and the result is that they were not pure, they
were not patriotic in that organization, and two of
them are under sentence to death at this moment."

This of course was completely false, though the
falsehood may presumably be charged to General
Hurley's defective memory. Julius and Ethel Rosenberg, sentenced to death, did their spying (as Fuchs
did practically all of his) when the atomic-energy
program was operated by the Manhattan Engineering District under General Groves—two years or
more before the Atomic Energy Commission (which
had received the "certificate of purity" that Hurley
mentioned) was established; indeed before it was
even thought of. Furthermore, the Rosenbergs never
worked even for Groves, let alone for the Atomic
Energy Commission. Yet a prominent man had said
that in an important hearing, so it was news; it ran
in one or more editions of the evening papers, and
doubtless on some news broadcasts, before it was corrected.

Who should have corrected it? Well, you would
think any senator would remember that Hurley was
completely wrong; but nobody said so. Two members of the committee who certainly knew, Senators
McMahon and Hickenlooper, happened not to be in

the committee room when Hurley made the statement. McMahon was told about it, came back while Hurley was still on the stand and managed to get it into the record that Hurley had made "a downright misstatement of facts." That duly got into the newspapers and on the radio; a senator had said it, so it was news.

Any competent news editor must have known that it was a downright misstatement of facts; yet I doubt if there was a newspaper in the country, printing Hurley's statement before McMahon's correction, that followed it with a bracketed insert, "This is not so." To do that would have been editorializing, interpreting the news, failing in objectivity. You could do it to Stalin and Hitler in their day, but tradition forbids doing it to one of our fellow citizens when he is engaged in controversy. Failure to make such a correction may salve a man's conscience about his loyalty to the ideal of objectivity. But how about his loyalty to the reader, who buys a newspaper thinking (or at least hoping) that it will tell him the truth? The newspaper is not giving him his money's worth if it tells him only what somebody says is the truth, which is known to be false.

It was the realization that objectivity had leaned so far over backward that it had become unobjective

162

which led to the rise of the syndicated newspaper column, and a little later of the radio news commentary. These are both news and interpretation; our listeners, or readers, understand that we are saying, "This is the news and this is what I think it means." But even for us, with much more latitude than the ordinary reporter, it is becoming harder and harder to get at the three-dimensional truth in Washington—partly because the news becomes more and more complex, partly because so much of it is coming to consist of never-ending serial melodramas, like soap operas on the radio, or those newspaper cartoon strips that used to be comic.

Especially is this true of Congressional committee hearings, where the same witnesses appear and reappear. Adequate coverage of such stories entails reporting not only what a man says now, but the very different thing he may have said last year—or last week.

Most people may remember that McCarthy said there are 205, or 57, or 81 Communists in the State Department. But this is only one of McCarthy's many self-contradictions; who can keep track of them all? I have a stack of his speeches two feet thick on my office shelf; but when he says something that stirs a vague recollection that he once said something very different, I seldom have time to run through his speeches. I can't afford to hire a full-time specialist to keep up with what McCarthy has said; and if I had a McCarthy specialist I should also have to hire a Louis Budenz specialist and a Harold Stassen specialist. For these favorite witnesses of Congressional committees (Stassen is a favorite no longer, now that he has a government job; but he was) are, like McCarthy, gifted with self-refreshing recollections; if the first story doesn't stand up, they have no trouble remembering something better. And their talents have been given an open field by that new doctrine of Congressional jurisprudence, perpetual jeopardy.

It was written into the Fifth Amendment to the Constitution that no man shall be subject, for the same offense, to be twice put in jeopardy of life or limb. The men who wrote that did not foresee that Congressional committees would take over much of the judicial process and would not be bound by the constitutional limitation since they deprive no man of life or limb—only (unless he is foolish enough to perjure himself, or to refuse to answer their questions) of his good name and his opportunity to earn a living. Acting on the principle that nothing is ever settled till it is settled right, they can disregard the fact that a man has been examined and found guiltless by another Congressional committee—or by more than one—not to mention grand juries, loyalty boards

164

and so on. They just keep on setting up committees till they find one that will get him.

Senator McCarran's Internal Security Committee seemed to have undertaken to correct any errors that anyone else may have made in the direction of leniency; and it carried on the good work by procedures that are, so far, novel and indeed unique—at least on this side of the Iron Curtain. A witness before the McCarran Committee—especially if he was a witness for the prosecution—knew what was expected of him. He didn't have to stop and think about his answer; it was usually handed to him wrapped up in the question: "You would say this is an indication of Communist sympathies, wouldn't you?" And this technique is made more effective by a new investigatory instrument known as the pertinent excerpt.

The pertinent excerpt is a refined and modernized version of our old friend, the sentence taken out of context. (One pertinent excerpt from a document used against Owen Lattimore turned out to be two sentences eleven pages apart, but put together.) Sometimes it is a line from a letter written fifteen years ago, read out of context to the man who wrote it (and didn't keep a carbon) with a demand that he explain what it means; but it is most effective when read to a man who didn't write it, indeed may never have seen it before, but is expected to say what it

165

means with no idea of the reasoning of which it was a part. How does he know—or how does a reporter know who is covering the hearing—that in context it might have a quite different meaning?

Some years ago Lattimore wrote a book called *Solution in Asia*. John Carter Vincent had read it—years ago. When the McCarran committee had Vincent on the stand they read him a number of pertinent excerpts from chapters about Mongolia and Chinese Turkistan—statements about Russia, which they kept trying to get him to stigmatize as party-line stuff; and eventually he had to say that some of it did seem to indicate an inclination toward Communism. Not till that evening, when Vincent had a chance to look at the book again, did he realize that these pertinent excerpts came from a chapter which began, "To all of these peoples Russia and the Soviet Union has a great attraction. *In their eyes*," etc. (The italics are mine, not the McCarran committee's; which omitted that phrase altogether.) They had seemed to be asking him about what Lattimore thought; actually they were asking him about what Lattimore believed other people thought. I had read that book—but years ago, and hurriedly, as I have to read most books; I had forgotten all about it, and I doubt if any other reporter at the hearing had read it at all. So the story had to go out that evening that

166

Vincent had found Communist leanings in Lattimore's book. Later, some admirers of the methods of the Mc-Carran committee seemed to suspect that this particular handling of a pertinent excerpt might be open to criticism. Irving Kristol, writing in the *Twentieth Century*, explained that Lattimore was merely putting his own opinions into the mouths of Uzbeks and Mongols, "secure in the knowledge that they were not likely to write a protesting letter to the *Times*." I do not know how Kristol can be sure of that; Lattimore was there and talked to those people, Kristol was not. But if the reader can be persuaded that Lattimore was only conducting a dialogue with himself, that might distract attention from the omission of some rather pertinent words from this pertinent excerpt. (One of the senators on the committee, when I questioned him after the hearing about the relevance of some of these excerpts, explained, "Well, the main thing was that we got Vincent to say something against Lattimore.")

I am not here concerned with the ethics of this sort of thing—though that is a topic on which much might be said—but with its effect on a reporter's endeavor to give the public a reasonably accurate story. Reporters covering the McCarran hearings were continually in danger of giving the public a false report, not of what was actually said in their presence but of

167

the three-dimensional truth of which what they hear is only one dimension. But who can read all the books or documents from which "pertinent excerpts" may be drawn? Who could remember them all, if he did?

William S. White of the New York *Times* happened to remember that there were material discrepancies, in emphasis if not in content, between General Wedemeyer's testimony before the McCarran committee and his testimony in the MacArthur hearings three months earlier—because White had covered them both and the memory had not had time to fade. What is remarkable about that episode is that the *Times* permitted White to report that discrepancy— something which many editors would regard as unobjective. But White seems to have more latitude than most reporters. Harold Stassen told the McCarran committee that at a conference of consultants to the State Department some years earlier, Lattimore had headed a "prevailing group" which recommended a ten-point program following the Communist line. When the stenographic record of the conference was published White analyzed it and demonstrated that there was hardly even a chemical trace of truth in Stassen's story. The *Times* published his analysis; few papers would.

But to analyze and find the truth requires not only

a good memory but time. How does the average reporter get at the truth in cases like this if he has to sit all day in a committee hearing and then come back and write his story, with no time to check up on the witness's past testimony or on the validity of the pertinent excerpts? How do I do it, compelled as I am to keep an eye on all the world's news, pouring in at the end of the day, besides the story that is right in front of me? Yet, unless we try it, we give the public only one dimension of the truth—a mere surface, under which something very different may lie concealed.

The McCarran committee was very sensitive to anything that might seem an imputation against its motives. I know nothing of its motives; what concerns me is that its procedures made it extremely difficult for reporters to find out the truth and pass it on to the public. Objectivity requires me, however, to report that those procedures have been praised by many people, including the Daughters of the American Revolution and (though somewhat absent-mindedly) the American Bar Association.

I have dwelt at length on the McCarran committee because it was a remarkable phenomenon and so far unique. (Under Jenner its proceedings have not been quite so raw.) But it is not the only committee

169

whose doings have encouraged, in reporting, another habit that is likely to mislead the public—the use of loaded words. One of those loaded words is "named." Now when a man is named as a Communist by Budenz, or named as a grafter by some of the witnesses before committees investigating corruption, that means nothing at all without corroboration. Yet if that man keeps appearing in the news the tag will stick to him; he has been named. A defendant on trial before a Congressional committee does not often, any more, say anything; he admits it, he acknowledges it. I have seen stories that came pretty close to saying, "The witness admitted that last year Christmas came on December 25."

Yet, searching my conscience while I was compiling these criticisms of others, I had to realize that lately I used an unloaded word when a loaded one would have been more accurate. That loaded word is "lobbying." There is nothing at all illegitimate about lobbying; there can be lobbying for good causes as well as bad, and by good or bad methods—though the most effective method, for the righteous as well as the wicked, is to convince a member of Congress that if he doesn't do what you want him to do, it will cost him votes. Nevertheless there has been so much lobbying for bad causes, by bad methods, that the word has become loaded; it means something evil.

170

The most effective job of lobbying that was done on Capitol Hill in 1952—out in the open, anyway—was done by the Citizens Committee for the Hoover Report, in persuading the Senate to accept the President's plan to put the Bureau of Internal Revenue under civil service. I happened to be in favor of that reform, as well as most of the recommendations of the Hoover Report; and when I reported these operations of the Citizens Committee, subconsciously realizing that "lobbying" has become a four-letter word, I said that they had reasoned with the senators. But I am afraid that if this had been an outfit that I didn't like, working for a measure I didn't favor, I should have called its operations lobbying—which they were. *Mea culpa;* I shall try to reform, and lead a better life.

One more example, which shows how the complexity of the news can lead to downright though quite unintentional misrepresentation. There are no more honest newspapers in the country than the New York *Times* and *Herald Tribune* and the Washington *Post* —perhaps no better newspapers either. Yet one morning in 1951 they all made the same mistake—and a mistake which happened to give support to their editorial policies. General Marshall had been testifying in the MacArthur hearings about MacArthur's personal and unilateral peace proposal of March 1951; and the next morning the top line of the *Times's*

171

eight-column head told us, "Marshall Says MacArthur Upset Peace Move"; and the eight-column heads were substantially the same in the *Post* and *Herald Tribune*.

Now General Marshall hadn't said that; he had said that MacArthur had lost "whatever chance there may have been" of making peace at that time. This verbatim quotation appeared in the lead of every story, of course; but there was room in the headline only for a very misleading simplification. Misleading because actually the chance of making peace at that time was infinitesimal—almost nonexistent. There was no agreement among the nations with troops in Korea as to what peace terms ought to be, and there is no indication that the Chinese ever even thought about it till they had taken a couple more first-class lickings. This fact was known to the State Department reporters for the *Post,* the *Times* and the *Herald Tribune,* but they weren't covering the MacArthur hearings; they were busy on their beats. It was not known to the men who were covering the hearings, or to the men who edited their stories, and it was nobody's business to tell them. I know of no newspaper which has a regular system of lateral internal communication by which one man tells another what he ought to know (unless they are both assigned to the same story); indeed he probably doesn't know the other man needs to know it. And news has become so complex that it is just good luck if any one man knows all he should know to cover his story properly.

There was of course far graver distortion of the testimony in the MacArthur hearings in some other newspapers. I have selected this instance only because the papers involved are technically among our best and ethically above suspicion of slanting the news to support their editorial policies. Yet that is what, quite inadvertently, they did.

What to do? More and more, from inside as well as outside the trade, there is a demand for interpretive reporting, which puts into the one-dimensional story the other dimensions that will make it approximate the truth. But this entails serious dangers. I have seen some undeniably well-intentioned endeavors to put in those other dimensions, but the dimensions were derived not from the evidence but from the opinions or prejudices of the reporter; and if the practice were to become general they might in some cases be derived from the opinions and prejudices of the publisher, as they so often used to be. One Chicago *Tribune* is enough. And even if a man's conscience is as rigorous, his mind as relentlessly objective, as the weights and measures in the Bureau of

173

Standards, he may still fall short of doing as accurate a job as he means to do because he doesn't know all the angles, or hasn't time to get around to them under the pressure of covering what is in front of him and writing a story about it.

No wonder then that editors are slow to accept the need of interpretation. In the fall of 1951 Senator Alexander Smith of New Jersey, a very moral and religious man, was a member of a subcommittee passing on the fitness of persons nominated as delegates to the United Nations Assembly, including Philip Jessup. McCarthy and Stassen had accused Jessup of Communist affiliations and sympathies; and after two weeks of hearings, the committee rejected Jessup by a vote of three to two. Senator Smith said he had absolute confidence in Jessup's ability, integrity and loyalty; he explicitly repudiated any belief in the charges against him; yet, because Jessup was a "controversial figure" and for other reasons quite irrelevant to the issues before the committee, he voted against Jessup and for McCarthy.

The committee approved the appointment of Dr. Channing Tobias, Negro religious leader, against whom similar charges had been brought; he admitted that he was a joiner and had sometimes been careless about what he joined; but he brandished the Negro vote at them. Whether there is a Negro vote is open

174

to doubt, but senators scare easily. It is impossible to escape the conclusion that Jessup too would have been approved if he had only been black.

One of the best reporters in Washington thought of beginning his report of that episode: "Yesterday afternoon Senator Alexander Smith wrestled with his conscience. He won." He didn't write that because he was afraid his paper wouldn't print it. But it might have printed it; in any case it seems to me an objective report of what happened. It is unthinkable that so high-minded a man as Senator Smith would have come to such a decision without wrestling with his conscience, and he certainly pinned it to the mat. Yet it could be argued that if that had been printed, it might have encouraged more freewheeling interpretation by reporters of less ability or less integrity.

The good newspaper, the good news broadcaster, must walk a tightrope between two great gulfs—on one side the false objectivity that takes everything at face value and lets the public be imposed on by the charlatan with the most brazen front; on the other, the "interpretive" reporting which fails to draw the line between objective and subjective, between a reasonably well-established fact and what the reporter or editor wishes were the fact. To say that is easy; to do it is hard. No wonder that too many fall back on the incontrovertible objective fact that the Honorable

John P. Hoozis said, colon quote—and never mind whether he was lying or not.

Yet more and more newsmen, in press and radio both, are coming to realize that we ought to do better than we are doing; and some of them are doing something about it. Dean Gordon Sabine of the University of Oregon School of Journalism has observed that the rise of McCarthy has compelled newspapers of integrity to develop a form of reporting which puts into context what men like McCarthy have to say. "Reporting all the dimensions of the news," he said, "we used to think of as dangerous. Today the lack of it creates the danger. And if this new approach brings the editorial page to the front page, if it mixes interpretation with naked fact, then we must realize simply that today we recognize the complexity of the news much more clearly than we did thirty or forty years ago, and we recognize the need for more capable newsgatherers and writers, and even more intelligent deskmen and editors."

We do indeed. A man who can be trusted with interpretive reporting must have both integrity and intelligence; even the New York *Times* seems to allow few if any of its reporters (except in the Sunday think-piece section) the freedom of interpretation that it accords to Bill White. Palmer Hoyt, publisher of the Denver *Post,* has issued to his staff a memorandum on how to treat the news about McCarthy so that the customers will not be deceived. "Many charges made by reckless or impulsive public officials," he says, "can not and should not be ignored; but news stories and headlines can be presented in such a manner that the reading public will be able to measure the real worth or value and the true meaning of the stories." A principle which he works out in some detail; "we are anxious," he says, "to take every possible step to protect the innocent."

And not merely the innocent victim of McCarthy, but the innocent consumer, who has little or no means of evaluating what he sees in print. All of us in the news business ought to remember that our primary responsibility is to the man who buys his newspaper, or turns on his radio, expecting us to give him in so far as is humanly possible not only the truth and nothing but the truth, but the whole truth.

IV

History in Doublethink

HOW long will these ex-Communists and ex-sympathizers abuse the patience of the vast majority which had sense enough never to be Communists or sympathizers at all? They have a constitutional right, of course, to tell us what we must do to be saved—as they have always done. Twenty years ago they were telling us the direct opposite of what they tell us now; but they were just as sure then as now that they had the sole and sufficient key to salvation and that those who did not accept it were forever damned. One becomes bored.

The arrogance of the ex-Communists is the most irritating thing about them, but not the most dangerous; and for that arrogance they have, in this country, official countenance. Congressional committees always seem willing to take the word of an ex-Communist—provided he has become a reactionary—against that of a man who never was a Communist. This preference may seem in contradiction to the stringent provisions of the McCarran Internal Security Act against the admission into this country of ex-Communists from abroad; but those provisions are only a phase of the protective tariff. The lucrative home market for exposures and revelations must be protected for domestic industry against the pauper labor of Europe. With this Congressional benediction there is some excuse for the ex-Communists to think they are a superior species.

But they thought that when they were Communists too; through a hundred-and-eighty-degree turn in their opinions they have clung to this certainty of their superiority to the unsaved—and to the concomitant certainty that their dogmas, whatever they may be, are complete, perfect and infallible. This is the mark of the *anima naturaliter totalitariana;* for I suspect it is not so much that Communism is an ineradicable taint, its aftereffects lingering in the system after the patient appears to be completely cured, as that it is people of this habit of mind who are most likely to become Communists. It is no accident that so many ex-Communists have become extreme reactionaries; it is remarkable only that some few of them have escaped into sanity. Aside from these saving few, Communist and ex-Communist are only species of the same genus; and I do not see why we should pay any more attention to them now than we did then.

For it is worth remembering, and worth reminding the young—before the ex-Communists pervert history any further—that not very many people did pay attention to them, even twenty years ago when what was then the American way of life (many people thought it was the only way) had come pretty close to breakdown. Some few thought they had found the answer in Technocracy, a somewhat more numerous few in Communism; but most people preferred to try another of the American ways of life; in the Presidential election of 1932 the Communists got a hundred thousand votes out of forty million. In the "intellectual" world the infection was stronger than elsewhere, yet even this turned out to be no more than a temporary nuisance. It spoiled some potentially good writers, it made considerable noise for a while; but it passed like any other fad, leaving as perhaps its principal legacy the angry writings of ex-Communists turned reactionary, who are still telling us what we must do to be saved. Where is their claim to authority? Not in their record.

But they seem able to persuade some people who were not there that their aberration was an all but universal aberration. Whittaker Chambers tells us that "from 1930 on a small intellectual army passed over to the Communist party." So it did, and a small army can look like a large army to a man who is in the midst of it; marching in step with his comrades, he might never notice the far larger army on the next road that is headed in the other direction. Alistair Cooke, who was not among us in those days, thought that in Alger Hiss a generation was on trial. That was not true even of his generation of "intellectuals"— not even of young intellectuals who graduated from college, looked around them and could see no jobs. Some of them fell for Communism; most did not. I suspect that Cooke's friends include some ex-Communists who cannot bring themselves to admit that their error was at all unusual; who must persuade others, as they have already persuaded themselves, that if minds of their quality were deluded, all other minds must have been deluded too.

Deceiving others is not yet too easy; men may write books and editorials and magazine articles, but evidence to the contrary is still available in the libraries. The first essential is to deceive one's self; and that, to the totalitarian mind (whether Communist or ex-Communist), offers little difficulty.

Control of the past depends above all on the training of memory. To make sure that all written records agree with the orthodoxy of the moment is merely a mechanical act. But it is also necessary

181

to remember that events happened in the desired manner. And if it is necessary to rearrange one's memories or to tamper with written records, then it is necessary to forget that one has done so.

So wrote Emmanuel Goldstein in *The Theory and Practice of Oligarchical Collectivism* (quoted by George Orwell in *1984*). This, of course, is the well-known art of Doublethink; Communists have to learn it, and ex-Communists find it hard to forget. And those of them who have bounced back all the way from one extreme to the other find it easier to keep practicing Doublethink because there is one cardinal principle that they have carried with them. They used to tell us that black was white, and damn us for doubting them. Now they admit it is black; but then and now they insist that there is no such thing as gray. If this requires a man to misread history, that is a small matter, so long as it enables him to retain confidence in his own intellectual integrity. And it would be unfair to say that he tries to persuade others to misread history; he remembers that events happened in the desired manner.

These reflections are obviously evoked by the great hullabaloo over *Witness* and will, I presume, be denounced as part of the "moral lynching" of Whittaker Chambers. Well, on the evidence as known, I think

182

Chambers told the truth about his relations with Hiss; I incline to believe him (with some reservations) about most of the other people with whom he claims to have been involved in subversive activities; and he writes with cogency and authority about the strange and turbid inner world of Whittaker Chambers. But he seems to have understood very little of what was going on around him, as is amply proved by his misinterpretations of history. A man who felt that he was returning in 1938 to the same world he had left in 1925, and who seems seriously to have accepted the suggestion that the Roosevelt administration might have him shot, had little awareness of objective reality.

The reason of course is obvious: Communism and the reaction from Communism had been the great fact in Chambers' life; it was inconceivable to him that it was not the great fact, if not in the life of all other individuals, at least in that of the society in which he existed. He quotes, and accepts, Krivitzky's remark that "there are only revolutionists and counter-revolutionists"—which Chambers underlines by adding that "in action, there is no middle ground." Yet one of the most protuberant facts of the history of the past twenty years is that there is a middle ground, and that in America and Western Europe the people who hold that middle ground have de-

183

feated both extremes. This is a matter of record; but since it doesn't fit in with the divinely handed-down interpretation of history it is necessary to remember that events happened in the desired manner, regardless of the facts.

Greater men than Chambers share this habit of mind. I do not suppose that John Dos Passos was ever a Communist; but certainly his sympathies, twenty or thirty years ago, were as near to the red end of the spectrum as they are now to the ultra-violet. At each end, he looked at the world through the appropriately colored glasses—which accounts for his seeing many things so clearly and not seeing many other things at all. He now feels that "we live in a society dedicated to its own destruction. How can it be," he asks, "that in a few short years we have sunk so low?" The answer is easy: we haven't—except in the opinion of a man who, instead of contrasting 1952 with 1932, merely contrasts his own ideologies of those years.

By coincidence there appeared in print, at about the same time as Dos Passos' melancholy views, a magazine advertisement which shares his opinion and even echoes his words. "We blush for America," said this advertisement; "for to what heights have we risen that we can fall so low?" The particular fall deplored by the advertiser was the repudiation of the terms extorted from General Colson on Koje Island by the kidnapers of General Dodd. This advertisement was signed by a business establishment, and it is perhaps only another coincidence that its address was right around the corner from Communist headquarters and its argument closely followed the current Communist line about Korea. But the touch of Doublethink was on it; and so it is on Dos Passos' concept of the present state of the nation.

Give Dos Passos credit for courage, however—more courage than most of the genuine blown-in-the-glass ex-Communists display. "If," he says, "the United States is doomed by forces of history too great for us to overcome, we will at least go down fighting." The people whose side he is on now have been going down fighting for the last twenty years—in 1932, when they predicted that grass would grow in the streets if Roosevelt were elected; in 1936, when the Liberty League demanded liberty for Du Ponts; and ever since—until 1952, when they were able to ride back in on the coattails of a man of very different type. But—though Dos Passos appears not to have noticed it—they didn't go down before the Communists. Chambers and Dos Passos have both been at, or near, both ends of the spectrum; at both ends, their thinking was of the same type; and at both ends, Roosevelt licked them. No wonder they detest his memory.

A dozen years ago, when Dos Passos was indulg-
ing in a brief interlude of objectivity before going the
rest of the way from one extreme to the other, he
wrote that "the history of the political notions of
American intellectuals during the past twenty years
is largely a record of how far the fervor of their hopes
for a better world could blind them to the realities
under their noses." The disappointment of those hopes
blinds them still; they admit now that black is black,
not white; but they insist that gray is black, too. I
can venture these criticisms of Dos Passos, for some
of whose gifts I have much admiration, in the confidence that they will not disturb him at all; he has
discounted all criticism beforehand. He is pretty sure
that "the 'liberals' who control communications in
the press and the radio and the schools and the colleges in this country have already crawled under the
yoke of the Communist party"; we are not dues-pay-
ing members (maybe he thinks we are too parsimoni-
ous) but we are the dupes of a sinister hoax. Thus
lightly to dismiss all contrary opinion no doubt helps
a man to feel comfortable inside himself; but I do
not think it makes him a very useful guide to the
people—a vast majority—who are not blind to the
realities under their noses.

A curious thing about these ex-Communists is that
they seem to derive a melancholy satisfaction from
the conviction that they are on the losing side. A

186

non-Communist Chinese, just at present, might be excused for thinking so; but there is no evidence for it in American history, except as rewritten by Doublethink. I suspect the answer is that they are naturally religious, temperamentally inclined to view the world in terms of catastrophe and apocalypse; someday the heavens will be rolled up like a scroll; *Dies irae, dies illa, solvit saeclum in favilla;* and they can view this with equanimity, since their personal salvation is secure. But once again, this makes them undependable guides for the vast majority which believes—as the vast majority of Americans has believed throughout our history, and has repeatedly proved—that something can be done about it, even if not so much as could be wished.

And the essential damage that could be done by these totalitarian thinkers—totalitarian no matter which end of the spectrum they may be on—would be to convince other people that there is no use trying to do anything about it; that those who are trying are only crypto-Communists even if they may not know it. A notable example is Chambers' comments on the New Deal revolution—which, as he and Senator Taft agreed, was a Socialist revolution in the name of liberalism. It has been amply pointed out that people who call it that do not know what Socialism means; but Chambers does indeed hit its essential point when he calls it "a shift of power from business

187

to Government." It was that, and I happen to believe that was a good idea—always provided that you do not give excessive power to Government, as we have not. (Even Chambers has to acknowledge that it was Government, after all, which convicted Hiss.)

Chambers apparently does not approve of that shift, and thinks we were better off when business had the power. It is the privilege of any citizen to think so; but when he says "it was a struggle for revolutionary power, which in our age is always a struggle for control of the masses," he confuses, or is likely to make his readers confuse, two kinds of revolutions carried out by two different methods. The Roosevelt revolution was the sixth we have had; and like all the others, it stopped before it went too far. There was a revolution in the early days of independence, a counter-revolution in 1787, a counter-counterrevolution in 1800; none of them found it necessary to resort to the guns of a cruiser, the dispersal of an elected assembly by bayonets, or the mechanisms of the police state. We had another partial revolution in Jackson's day; still another, begun by the Congressional elections of 1866 and consummated twenty years later by the Supreme Court's decision that the Fourteenth Amendment protects corporations, transferred power from Government to business. The Roosevelt revolution merely reversed that. Chambers has a right to

188

dislike the reversal, but when he implies that the Roosevelt revolution and Communist revolution differed only in degree, whosoever is deceived thereby is not wise.

All these are matters of record and will remain so unless—which I do not expect—the Doublethinkers get control of the country and "make sure that all written records agree with the orthodoxy of the moment." Until then, they are more of a nuisance than a menace—as they were in the days when they thought that salvation was to be found in Moscow. They are religious people; as Arthur Schlesinger, Jr., has pointed out, a man may be religious without feeling certain that he has the complete and unalterable final truth and that those who disagree with him are damned in time and in eternity. But these people must feel that. Some of them, finding that final truth is not in Moscow, have sought and found it in Rome; hardier characters become their own Popes and are just as sure of their own infallibility as they were in the days when they parroted the resolutions of the Comintern.

There is another kind of thinking, which some religious people find not inconsonant with their view of the relations between man and God. I described it in the *Saturday Review* twenty years ago and it seems pertinent to quote that description now:

To admit that there are questions which even our so impressive intelligence is unable to answer, and at the same time not to despair of the ability of the human race to find, eventually, better answers than we can reach as yet—to recognize that there is nothing to do but keep on trying as well as we can, and to be as content as we can with the small gains that in the course of ages amount to something—that requires some courage and some balance.

That kind of thinking has played a great part in American history, from Benjamin Franklin down to John Dewey; and it has worked. But the Communists against whom I was writing then had no use for it, nor have most of them now that they are ex-Communists. There must be a final truth and they must have it; experimental thinking is only a groping in the dark. And if its successes are written in the record of American history from Jefferson (yes, and Hamilton) through Lincoln down to Franklin Roosevelt, that fact can be obliterated by remembering that events happened in the desired manner—by knowing that press and radio and schools and colleges are all controlled by the Communists and that the Roosevelt administration had its critics shot.

I repeat—one becomes bored.

V

Grandeurs and Miseries
of Old Age

I AM almost sixty-four years old. That is not very old by modern standards, especially in a country whose benevolent government urges on me the advantages of being older still. When I am sixty-five, the Bureau of Internal Revenue assures me, I shall be able to deduct another $600 from my taxable income; and if I have the additional felicity to become blind, I can deduct some more.

I have no ambition to go blind at any age, despite this allurement; for that matter I am not anxious to be sixty-five, though I shall be unless I die pretty soon. My fan mail includes a good many gleeful predictions that I am going to be lynched; but barring that misfortune, I ought to be good for another ten or fifteen years if there is anything in the doctrine of hereditary longevity. But no matter how long I may last I am not persuaded that the best is yet to be, even

191

by Catherine Drinker Bowen's eloquent disquisition in *Harper's* on the magnificence of age. I recognize and applaud her endeavor to reassure us that what is going to happen to all of us, whether we like it or not, is really something pretty good; but I cannot feel that the general public can draw much encouragement from the truly magnificent old age of the various worthies she mentions, notably Mr. Justice Oliver Wendell Holmes.

It is no doubt true, as she says, that "luck being equal, whether a man at eighty finds himself reaping the harvest or the whirlwind depends on how he has spent his forties and thirties and twenties." But luck is not equal; and it may be that to be an Oliver Wendell Holmes or a John Dewey at ninety you had to be a Holmes or a Dewey from the start, both in physical constitution and in potential mental capacity.

I once asked John Dewey how he maintained such intellectual and physical activity at an advanced age, and he said that when you have survived a childhood in Vermont you can take just about anything that happens to you afterward. I have no statistics on the juvenile mortality in Vermont in the eighteen-sixties; no doubt all those who survived were tough, but they were not all Deweys. I have a friend aged eighty-four who is better than I am; but to judge from the record she always was, at any age.

To feel that Mrs. Bowen has been overly optimistic

192

is not to accept the dark view of old age held by the author of Ecclesiastes; but that is partly because medical science has made considerable advances since his day. Considerable, but not yet enough. When the grinders cease because they are few, the dentist can replace them; when eyes that look out of the windows be darkened, the oculist can take effective measures. But who can give us back those elastic arteries? (Since writing the foregoing, I have happily discovered that Bourbon retards their ossification.) No doubt in due time the doctors can take care of that and can correct the other deteriorations that now commonly come with advancing years. Some writers have looked forward to the time when men and women will be potentially immortal and will voluntarily retire from life only when they have seen everything and become bored with repetitions. When that happy day comes, Mrs. Bowen's argument will be more persuasive than it is now. In the meantime there is no use kidding ourselves that every man who lives into the late eighties or the nineties can be an Oliver Wendell Holmes, or a John Dewey, or an Arturo Toscanini, no matter how rectitudinously he may have behaved while he was still young enough to have some choice about it. If there be consolations to offset the inevitable physical decay that befalls most of us, they ought to be more generally applicable.

Public life seems to be a pretty good preservative—

if not for Presidents, at least for Congressmen who
work about as hard as Presidents, though they have
less responsibility. Chairman Robert L. Doughton of
the House Ways and Means Committee—one of the
most exacting as well as most important committees of the Congress—retired in 1952 at the age of
eighty-eight because he was afraid he was getting old
and might be not quite so good as he used to be; to
everybody else he looked just about as good as ever,
which was pretty good. Chairman Adolph J. Sabath
of the House Rules Committee was cut off untimely
at eighty-six; but he had worn himself out by twenty
years of fighting with the beasts at Ephesus—the reactionary majority of his committee. (The successor
to his seat in the House is only seventy-eight, which
gives him time to mature.) Senator Theodore Francis
Green, at eighty-six, is about as lively, mentally and
physically, as any man on Capitol Hill, though last
year his doctors told him that he would have to stop
high-diving. Some people worry because the fate of
the world appears to depend in large degree on Winston Churchill, aged seventy-nine, and Konrad Ade-
nauer, aged seventy-eight. But there is a good chance
that men who have lasted as long as that may still
have some more years of work left in them.

But these men are exceptions, as much as the
Franklins and Palmerstons and Gladstones who in

194

past generations kept going long after most men had run down. They offer no great encouragement to the average man.

Perhaps in this matter there is no such thing as the average man. It is common knowledge that some people grow old faster than others, and not till lately has there been official demarcation of the frontier between youth and age. In the fall of 1953 the President said that one reason he appointed Earl Warren as Chief Justice was "his relative youth"—sixty-two. On the same day the Governor of Puerto Rico pardoned a prisoner on account of "his advanced age"— sixty-three. Between those two years, then, must lie the Great Divide, though I seem to have been working so hard that I never noticed it when I passed over it.

But in their relation to old age men differ vastly not only in their abilities and their physical strength, but economically and occupationally. If the insurance companies can be believed, I cannot say much about the average man either; for they tell us, or used to tell us, that 99 per cent of all men of my age are dependent on their children, or pensions, or charity. And even among the one per cent of us who can still make a living there are differences—for instance, whether we are responsible only for ourselves or for

195

organizations and institutions. Most of us in my business, the news business, are responsible only for ourselves; in my particular branch of it there are three men who are ten years older than I am and still going strong; and one of the greatest of editorial writers, the late E. M. Kingsbury, was still at it when he was ninety. But if one of us should go haywire, he could be bounced out with no loss to anybody but himself. The danger that men in responsible executive positions might go haywire is the most serious hazard of old age.

The steady physical deterioration that afflicts most of us is deplorable, but so long as it remains merely physical it is not disastrous. Far worse is the danger that in advanced years a man's mind might go back on him at some unpredictable moment and drive him to make mistakes that would have been unthinkable a year or two earlier. That is why some of our aged statesmen, to all appearance as good as ever, nevertheless find it advisable to retire before that unforeseeable day when all at once they will not be as good as ever, or good at all. Some of them do not retire; Gladstone was beginning to slip, physically at least, in his last ministry, though he saw it and left office before the consequences became too serious. Hindenburg, elected president of the German Reich at seventy-seven, hoped (so Walter Goerlitz tells us) that he would not be left in office till he became senile;

196

"for one never knows one's self when that is happening." He was left in office; it happened, but he did not know it was happening; and that was one of the reasons for the downfall of the German Republic.

The older a man grows, the greater the danger that this will happen to him. Against this and minor miseries of age, what are the offsets? Not all, I am afraid, that have sometimes been recommended. Much has been written about the joys of calm contemplation, in old age, of a long and honorable life. But it is a rare man, unless he has great skill at self-deception, who can review a career, however bespangled with good deeds and glory, without his eye's lighting on something that could have been done otherwise and better, and might have made a considerable difference if it had been done better; but it is too late to do anything about it now. The pleasure in such retrospection seems to me by no means unalloyed.

They tell us too of the joy of seeing long endeavor come to ultimate fruition. Well—— Back in the eighties a young actor named Frank Bacon was playing in California vaudeville with his wife. They had a baby, and like many young couples they needed more money than they had. But then he had an Idea—an idea that might make enough money, and win enough fame, to solve all their problems; an idea for a play about a hotel on the state line, half in Nevada and half in California, and combining (as

197

the late Frank Munsey might have said) the best features of both. He finally got it written—with what effort, and what joy, only the amateur writer knows—and sent it off to a producer (or maybe an agent) in New York. And nothing happened.

It made the rounds of the New York producers, and nothing continued to happen. Meanwhile Bacon and his wife continued to play in vaudeville, and made a living; the baby grew older; with pain, Bacon cut down the play that embodied the Idea into a vaudeville act, which kept them afloat. But it was a long way from California vaudeville to the glories of Broadway; he still hoped for better things, still kept sending the play around—and at last a producer took it. He gave it to the best play doctor of the time for reworking; it was produced on Broadway, with Bacon playing the lead; it ran longer than any play had ever run in New York up to that time, and he made a million dollars out of it—when he was sixty-four.

I heard Frank Bacon tell that story in 1918, and he finished, "Anyway, I can still use the money." He probably used it more wisely at sixty-four than he would have at thirty-four, but he didn't get so much fun out of it; nor was there anything like so much of it, for the income tax was terrific in 1918 and unheard of in the eighties. Nor could any joy that comes to a man with thirty years' more experience approximate the emotion of the beginning author who slips into the mail the manuscript that embodies his Great Idea. After thirty years he may even have come to doubt its greatness.

It has been argued that in old age most of your troubles are behind you. The late Don Marquis once wrote that when you have reached the age of fifty-five, everything has happened to you that can happen; you are no longer in danger of being devastated by something new. He was wrong. Before he was fifty-five he had had about as much bad luck as any man I ever knew, but after that he had some more—a stroke which laid him flat on his back for the last two years of his life, conscious, but unable to do or even to say anything about it.

There is also mere curiosity. I hope to keep on living for a while to see what happens, but I realize that I may not like it at all. Abraham Lincoln, if he had lived another ten years, would have had a very poor opinion of what the United States had become; but it is always possible that with his tremendous personal prestige and his unequaled political skill he might have prevented it from becoming what it was by 1875. Lesser men can have no such expectation.

There is, however, one offset to the inevitable infirmities, at least for us of the one per cent who have been lucky enough to be able to keep our noses above water; and that is freedom—freedom from the passions of youth. I don't mean what you mean; from that particular passion, I should imagine, few men or women are ever happy to be set free. We read in the pages of history that Sophocles the tragic poet, at the age of eighty-nine, was asked by some impertinent young squirt if he were still able to enjoy the pleasures of love. "My friend," said Sophocles solemnly, "I give thanks to the gods every day that I have been freed from that tyrannous desire." It is, however, the general opinion of men old enough to have an opinion that Sophocles was merely making the best of a bad job—whistling in the graveyard of his capacities.

The dominant passion of most young men—and middle-aged men, for that matter—is a lust for Success; they bend most of their efforts toward making a name, or a fortune, or both. But the time comes when they have either made it or not, and it is too late to do much more about it. Accordingly—always provided you have done well enough to keep afloat— ambition fades away; you no longer give a damn, or at any rate not much of a damn.

This too needs qualification, in both directions. A senator who in his eighties is defeated—as several senators have been—for re-election to a seat that he has held for thirty years probably feels even worse about it than he would have felt thirty years earlier; and those unfortunate novelists who under some obscure compulsion still push out a book a year, long after they have nothing left to say, probably hate unfavorable reviews just as much as they did in their youth.

Nor can you ever be quite sure when a man is through. Winston Churchill, at sixty-two, was a failure. He had been, at times, a considerable figure in each party, but now he was out of both parties; he had just tried to organize a King's party to support Edward VIII in the abdication crisis and had failed not only immediately but rather ludicrously; he told his friends that he was done for. Three years later he was called on to save his country, and he did it.

But not many of us are Churchills, any more than we are Lincolns. Nevertheless we of the one per cent can savor the sense of freedom that comes from the disappearance of ambition. When we were younger, getting and spending we laid waste our powers—and sometimes, in the headlong drive for success, some of us were in danger of laying waste something still more important, our conscience. A good many young men have sometimes been confronted with something that they know they ought to do; but if they did it, it might have an unfavorable if not a disastrous effect on their future. They should have done it any-

201

way, no doubt; but it is a good deal easier not to worry about the effect on your future when your future is behind you.

It is quite true that 'tis man's perdition to be safe when for the truth he ought to die—or, as the phrase is more likely to translate itself in these times, when for the truth he ought to lose his job, with small chance of getting another. But it is, emotionally if not ethically, a somewhat different matter to tell a young man with a wife and children whom he is barely able to support on his salary that for the truth, his wife and children ought to starve too. And that is a situation that increasingly comes up in the present drive, Congressional and local, against freedom of thought—particularly in the schools and colleges where above all freedom of thought must be preserved.

Professors and teachers in schools and colleges are, tempted to pull in their horns, to say nothing at all; otherwise their students, or their students' parents, might report them to the American Legion—as has happened—and any deviation from the norm of reactionary thinking will be regarded as subversion. With the result also, as Mrs. Roosevelt reported after her nation-wide travels in the winter of 1953, that the young people who are just coming up and see what is happening begin to be afraid to think and afraid to

202

act, for fear that something they may say or do now will be dug up and thrown at them twenty years later and ruin their careers. (Senator McCarthy has several times damned, or tried to damn, middle-aged men for what they did or said in college and have long since repudiated.) A despotism might be able to stand this loss of heart, though I doubt it; but a republic whose young people are in that state of mind is on its way downhill.

We have got to defeat this attack on the freedom of the mind; and I think we can defeat it if enough of us stand up against it—enough of all kinds of people, rich and poor, young and old. But it takes courage for a young man with a family to stand up to it; all the more obligation on those of us who have nothing left to lose. At any age it is better to be a dead lion than a living dog—though better still, of course, to be a living and victorious lion; but it is easier to run the risk of being killed (or fired) in action if before long you are going to be dead anyway. This freedom seems to me the chief consolation of old age.

VI

Are We Worth Saving?
And If So, Why?

A CENTURY or so ago a Harvard graduate wrote a hymn whose opening line, plausible enough when written, turned out to be one of the most inaccurate forecasts ever set down:

> The morning light is breaking,
> the darkness disappears.

The final couplet of that stanza, however, would—with the omission of a single word—be a fairly accurate picture of the world today:

> Each breeze that sweeps the ocean brings
> tidings from afar
> Of nations in commotion, prepared for
> Zion's war.

Commotion indeed; but it is not Zion's war for which they are preparing. Yet in his day the Reverend Samuel F. Smith seemed to have good reason for his confidence in the success of the missionary enterprises that were then spreading over the world, and not only in their direct success but in the derivative benefits that would flow from them. He had faith—not only faith in his religion; but back of that, like most men of his day, he had the general confidence of the Western world in that golden afternoon, the immensely successful nineteenth century; an assurance that it had not only a religion but a culture which was so good in itself that it was the Christian duty of all who possessed it to extend it to less favored races.

To its intended beneficiaries that assurance must often have seemed arrogance. Especially as expressed in the most famous missionary hymn of the time:

> By many an ancient river, from many a
> palmy plain,
> They call us to deliver their souls from
> error's chain.

The call was audible mostly to the inner ear, but there it rang loudly.

> Shall we whose souls are lighted by wisdom
> from on high,
> Shall we to men benighted the lamp of life
> deny?

Responding to that appeal, many men and women went forth into the foreign field, performed the most heroic, arduous and often hazardous labors, and sometimes laid down their lives. We owe them the utmost respect; yet I am sure we all wish that the appeal had been phrased more tactfully. The missionary techniques of Olaf Trygvasson no longer commend themselves; but at least, when he gave his subjects the choice between accepting the lamp of life and getting their throats cut, he didn't pretend that they had asked for it.

But Bishop Heber and the Reverend Samuel Smith profoundly believed what they wrote, as did most men of their time. The principal group that disagreed with them, the Hardshell Baptists, did so only in an even greater faith—that when God chose to save the heathen He could do it by Himself, without the help of contributors to foreign missions. Logically and theologically they seem to have had the better of the argument; but they were a feeble and dwindling group because the vast majority was inspired, for the most part unconsciously, by a faith which comprehended and transcended theology. The great Protestant missionary effort of the nineteenth century, like the great Catholic missionary effort of the sixteenth century, was the expression of a strong and vigorous culture— different phases only of the culture of what we call the Western world; though a Polynesian or even a Japanese might reasonably ask, West of what? In the sixteenth century the West was just awakening, with a delighted surprise, to an awareness of its own strength, which had seemed gravely in question in the opening phases of the Turkish onslaught. By the nineteenth century the West had no doubt that it was the culmination of all human progress to date, with even more dazzling achievements lying beyond.

In the middle of the twentieth century the principal questions in dispute among Western intellectuals seem to be whether the West can be saved, and if it is worth saving. The two most popular of recent historical philosophers both think the Western world is going downhill, and one of them seems to feel that it won't be much loss. Spengler appreciated the loss more than Toynbee; if he felt that it was inevitable, that was perhaps because he was an artist rather than a philosopher. Yet, though it may be only a coincidence, it is certainly a disquieting one that he and Toynbee, starting from very different premises, come out to about the same conclusion as to the phase of development that our civilization has reached; and still more disquieting, as to what lies ahead—what Spengler called Caesarism, and Toynbee the universal state.

There are optimists, of course, who think that a

207

really universal state—a world-wide state—could be created by some other means than military force; Spengler and Toynbee are not among them nor, to compare small things with great, am I. So long as Communists remain Communists any world coalition government would be subject to the same dangers, and likely to meet the same fate, as the coalition governments of Poland and Czechoslovakia; and there is still wisdom enough in the West not to run that risk. Others think that even if a universal state were created by military force the result would not be Caesarism—provided, of course, that our side won. A couple of years ago Bertrand Russell was one of these; lately he seems to have become discouraged, and offers us the variant but not very cheerful prospect of a dual Caesarism, with Premier Malenkov and President McCarthy dividing the world between them and collaborating to suppress dissent in both their realms. I do not suppose that Russell was entirely serious in suggesting this; he may only have been reading Orwell's *1984,* or he may have been reading the *Congressional Record.* Such a future seems improbable; but in the world we live in, no one can be sure that it is impossible.

Spengler is dead and can write no more; he has said his say; within his artistic scheme, the progressive deterioration of any culture seemed inevitable. Any man who keeps on writing and talking is likely to contradict himself; Toynbee has written so much that he has involved himself in about as many contradictions as Dr. John H. Watson, when he set down the history of Sherlock Holmes. A few years ago Toynbee seemed to have some hope that the creative minority of our civilization had not yet lost its creativity, not yet become a merely dominant minority, for the inadequacy of whose rule the internal proletariat would have to compensate by creating or adopting a universal religion; now he seems to think we have passed the point of no return. We passed it, apparently—or at least so he thought when he delivered the Reith Lectures last year; he may since have changed his mind again—we passed it toward the end of the seventeenth century, when men became disgusted with the endless religious wars which neither side ever decisively won, and turned to secular interests—turned from preoccupation with preparation for the next world to consideration of what could be done with this one; and, increasingly, to what could be done with it through technology.

And for this apostasy, thinks Toynbee, God has punished us—punished the West by the loss of the East; not only our territorial possessions and our commerce there but our moral influence in an East

209

which increasingly turns toward our Communist enemy. The East rejected our religion, and our technology with it, when they were parts of an indivisible
way of life; it accepted our technology when it was
divorced from our religion (and incidentally had become far more efficient; that is to say, far more worth
accepting) with consequences which became apparent at Pearl Harbor in 1941 and more recently in
Korea. "The fortunes," he says, "of Western civilization in the mission field veered right around from
conspicuous failures to conspicuous successes as soon
as its attitude toward its own ancestral religion had
veered around from a warm devotion to a cool skepticism." Which appears to mean, when the mission
field had become the field of a new kind of missionary,
offering no longer the lamp of life but oil for the
lamps of China, and all that went with it.

History does not support this interpretation. It has
been subjected to a number of searching criticisms—
notably by Professor Michael Karpovitch in the *New
Leader* and by G. F. Hudson in *Commentary*. Karpovitch, after pointing out that Toynbee is wrong on
all the things that Karpovitch knows most about,
suavely admits that no doubt he is right in other fields.
Hudson makes a more general attack on the entire
doctrine, to which a layman can offer only a couple
of corroborative footnotes. The great success of Prot-

210

estant missions—not to mention a vigorous revival of Catholic missions and the beginnings of the penetration of the East by Western technology as well—came at a time when the cool skepticism of the eighteenth century had been buried under a new wave of evangelical fervor, when Protestantism was not only as vigorous but as dogmatic as the Catholicism of the Counter-Reformation. (I do not know whether Toynbee regards Modernist Protestantism as a religion at all; but he can hardly deny that title to Fundamentalist Protestantism.)

What at present appears to be the failure of Protestantism in China seems to be due less to divine wrath at apostasy than to an intensified form of the thing that caused the eventual failure of Catholicism in Japan, when it had lost little if any of its energy and fervor in Europe—the fear of a suspicious and despotic government that religion had been merely the cover for imperialistic political intrigues. In either case there was little evidence on which to base that fear; but despots need little evidence—especially despots newly come to power, who still feel insecure.

It might indeed be argued that the West, in its relation with the East, is being punished for its sins. But the sin is not apostasy; it is too great faith. We have all observed that the sin that is most surely and sharply punished is a mistake—however well in-

211

tended, however it may have seemed at the time the thing to do. The punishment is often delayed, and falls on the descendants of those who made the mistake—often on innocent bystanders. "Those eighteen upon whom the tower of Siloam fell, and slew them— think ye that they were sinners above all men that dwelt in Jerusalem?" We are authoritatively assured that they were not. The sin was that of the architect or the contractor; the punishment fell on people who only happened to be around. Many Europeans and Americans have suffered in Asia, and may presently suffer in Africa, for mistakes for which they were in no way responsible—mistakes made from the highest motives, as a result of faith.

For alongside the theological religion of the West, which in the past two and a half centuries has had its ups as well as its downs, there was growing up in Western Europe and America a secular religion, held as fervently by devout Christians as by rationalists— the faith in freedom, in self-government, in democracy. (Indeed the only living ex-president of Columbia University has more than once implied that only believers in a theological religion can believe in this secular religion too. The evidence for this cannot be found in history.) The Westerners who interpenetrated the East in the nineteenth century, whether missionaries, engineers, businessmen or administrators, mostly carried this religion with them. They made many mistakes; but it was devotion to this secular religion that led them to make what, from the standpoint of practical consequences, was the worst mistake the West ever made in dealing with the East. They educated the natives.

Not merely in the operation of modern weapons, though they did that first, for the greater convenience of Western powers warring among themselves; these were men of faith, faith in the whole Western culture of which this secular religion was becoming steadily a more important part. Many of those whom they educated sprang from cultures far older than ours and in some respects more distinguished. But it was the Western culture that seemed to work, so it did not have to be forced on them; in this case they really did call us to deliver their minds, at least, from error's chain. We educated them in Western medicine and engineering, in Western government and law. And in the course of that education the pupils were exposed to the fact that there were such things as freedom and self-government and democracy— things which the educators obviously regarded as good for themselves; it was only a question of time till the pupils began to suspect that they might be good for everybody. Educate any man, of whatever race or color, in what he didn't know before and you are

213

taking a chance; how he will turn out will depend somewhat on the education but more on his background and environment and on what was in him to start with; you may get a Nehru and you may get a Jomo Kenyatta. The one thing they have in common is a conviction that those who educated them, having fulfilled that function, ought to get out.

I have enough faith in that secular religion to believe that in the long run the consequences of this will be beneficial—as they seem to be already in the successor states of the Indian Empire. But that is no consolation to those on whom various towers of Siloam have fallen elsewhere.

This digression was necessitated by the fact that the most popular of contemporary historians has offered an explanation not only for our unsatisfactory relations with Asia and Africa but for the general dilemma of our times—an explanation which not only to me but to many of my betters seems no explanation at all. But what then is the matter with us? What have we left, if anything, that is worth saving?

This first and obvious answer, of course, is "If we aren't worth saving, who is?" Faulty as we are, we seem infinitely preferable—by our standards—to the moral nihilism and intellectual rigidity of the Soviet system which is competing with us for the allegiance of the East; competing indeed, though with little success outside of France and Italy, for the allegiance of our own citizens. Unfortunately, we do not always seem preferable to those among whom our missionaries, and those of the opposition, are working; and if through force or deception they have once accepted the opposition's gospel, they find that the choice is irrevocable. Rebels on the barricades would be blown to pieces by tanks and bombing planes; indeed the secret police would never let anybody get to the barricades in the first place.

G. F. Hudson—following Orwell—holds that modern totalitarian techniques would make impossible even Toynbee's last refuge for the disconsolate, wheresoe'er they languish—the creation by the internal proletariat of a universal church to compensate for the shortcomings of a universal state. "If Nero," says Hudson, "had had the resources of the MVD at his disposal, the early Christians would have been publicly confessing how in their vileness they had set fire to Rome on instructions of the King of Parthia." In the world we live in, freedom once lost is lost to stay lost. We had better remember that, in dealing with our internal even more than with our external problems.

Granted, however, that from anything that could be called an ethical viewpoint we are better worth

215

saving than our adversaries, this is no proof that we are going to be saved unless we have the qualities that enable us to save ourselves. The western Roman Empire was far more worth saving than the barbarian tribal dominions that surrounded it and eventually overran it; but its own faults brought it down. This is worth mentioning since not only Spengler and Toynbee but lesser men have dealt with our predicament in terms of what befell civilizations of the past; and these analyses, however embellished with facts, or conjectures, from Chinese and Mayan and Sumerian history, all rest pretty much on the one case about which we have tolerably complete information—the decline and fall of the Roman Empire. Many historians have attempted to explain it; almost all of them, even Gibbon—even Rostovtzeff—seem to me to explain it largely in terms of their own experience, and observation of their own times.

I shall not add to that confusion, but shall only point out one or two details in which our situation is different. We know now that the happiness and prosperity of the age of the Antonines, which so impressed Gibbon, was only relative—considerable no doubt compared to what had gone before and what was to come afterward, but behind the splendid front there was a dry rot inside. Economically the Empire was deteriorating, and intellectually, too.

Economically the Western world is doing pretty well nowadays; and in the English-speaking and Scandinavian countries (Switzerland and the Low Countries as well) the problem that Rome never solved and that finally did more than anything else to bring Rome down has been solved with a fair degree of success—the problem of passing prosperity around, of seeing that everybody gets some of it. If France and Italy solved that problem too, the Communist parties in those countries would soon shrink to the hard core. Our civilization, said Rostovtzeff thirty years ago—lately echoed and emphasized by Professor Robinson of Brown—our civilization will not last unless it be a civilization not of one class but of the masses. This is a warning that might more pertinently be directed toward the Soviet Union than the United States, in so far as what exists in the Soviet Union can be called a civilization. As for Rostovtzeff's last despairing question, "Is not every civilization bound to decay as soon as it penetrates the masses?" we can only say that we shall in due course find out. We have started in that direction and we can't turn back.

The Romans, outside of the cities, never got started; and even there civilization was a narrowing pyramid, with a hollow top. The most notable thing about the age of the Antonines was its intellectual sterility, in a period of rest between calamities when the Western world might have made vast advances and fortified itself against the calamities that were to come—the classic case of what Toynbee calls the loss of creativity in the dominant minority. Are we losing it? Dr. J. G. de Beus of the Netherlands Embassy in Washington, who has lately analyzed these forecasts of the future, thinks the Western world is still vigorously creative—not only in science and technology but in politics, domestic and foreign, and in art and letters as well.

It is perhaps fortunate that this optimistic view was set down before the recent sculptural competition in London for a statue of the Unknown Political Prisoner, where the prize was given to a contraption in wire that looked like nothing, unless perhaps a television aerial. As for letters, most of the most admired literature of the Western nations—especially the English-speaking nations—for thirty-five years past has been to all appearance the effluvium of a sick society. English literature, between wars, gave us an almost unrelieved picture of a nation in process of dissolution from its own internal weakness—a nation that would collapse in ruins as soon as somebody pushed. But the time came when somebody pushed, and it did not collapse; indeed the people who did the pushing eventually did the collapsing too.

Many American novelists have written about the late war or about American society in the years just before it and since. Most of their works would be intelligible if written by Frenchmen after 1870, or Spaniards after 1898—mercilessly candid pictures of the inner decay that led to calamitous defeat. But since we happened to win the war, something seems to have been wrong with the picture—not perhaps with the individual picture which each man saw, but with the total picture which few of them ever noticed.

This phenomenon is a symptom of what has been called the alienation of "intellectuals" from the life around them, which is taken very seriously by many intellectuals. I cannot see that it makes much difference, with intellectuals like these. They wrote their books, which often sold widely; the society around them bought the books, read them and ignored them. Indeed their authors usually ignored them when the chips were down; men who had spent their lives proving that the United States was not worth fighting for went out and fought for it like everybody else.

This naturally does not mean that I share the scorn of Senator Ferguson and his type for eggheads, radical or otherwise. It depends on what you call an intellectual. Franklin and Jefferson were not alienated from the society around them, either in America or when they lived in France; yet they qualified as intellectuals in about the fastest company the world has known since Periclean Athens. It seems doubtful, however, if the more rigorous intellectuals of our time would acknowledge them as members of the club.

The first condition of the survival of any civilization is that it should win its wars. Rome did, till its armies wore themselves out fighting one another. I think that from the military point of view we could win the next war, if we should have to fight it, despite the weakness of our air defense in the northeastern approaches. But to win a war under modern conditions requires more than military strength—more even than preservation of a sound dollar. It requires political shrewdness, domestic and foreign, to a degree the Romans seldom had to practice. For five centuries after the battle of Magnesia they had virtually no need for a foreign policy, till the degenerate days when they found it necessary to make an alliance with one German tribe against another. The United States, as the *prima inter pares* of a coalition, has to deal with complexities convincingly set forth not long ago by the President, who has had more experience in dealing with coalitions than any other man since Metternich. It would not be easy to cope with them, even if he had the actual (though not the theoretical) power of a Roman Emperor; still less is it easy in a republic whose Constitution, as Woodrow Wilson once put it, permits the President to be as big a man as he can. If he cannot be or does not want to be a big man, there will be plenty of others who will volunteer to fill the vacancy. Every American President must conduct his foreign policy against and in spite of men who, if they no longer think we should not have a foreign policy at all, at least think it should not be his policy. In the circumstances, we have in recent years done remarkably well.

What a civilization like ours, which is not a universal state but a coalition of independent powers, can do to insure its own continuance depends quite as much on how each state manages its own internal affairs. Here the Romans met the proximate cause of their disaster. When they had a good man at the head of the state all went well—unless he was a good man like Antoninus Pius—perhaps the most virtuous of all rulers of a great realm and certainly pre-eminent in manly beauty, but he appears to have been only a glorified Calvin Coolidge, who sat there and went through the motions while the problems piled up for his unhappy successor. But when the Romans got a bad man in, there was no way to get him out except by assassination or revolution. Over a period of ninety years almost every Emperor—and they were many— was got out by one or the other of those methods— good men as well as bad.

The nations which embody Western civilization are

no longer subject to that danger, but their political systems have other defects. Mr. Walter Lippmann remarks that if the free world is in peril, it is not because our enemies are so strong but because the free nations are so badly governed; and they are badly governed because of the usurpation of power by the national legislatures. . . . Well—we must discriminate. In the nations of the British Commonwealth the supremacy of the legislature is the essence of their constitutions, and they have learned how to make it work. In the French Republic it is also the essence of the constitution; in the three quarters of a century of the Third and Fourth Republics they have not learned how to make it work. In our own republic it is in flat conflict with the Constitution, and no wonder it doesn't work. It is an old story; long before the recent publicized attacks on the State Department, and on the President's control of foreign policy, the principal problem of our government was Congressional usurpation, usually through committees, of executive functions. Congress not only tells administrators what they must do, which is its right, but how to do it, which is not its right and is wholly outside Congress's field of practical competence as well as of authority.

A Congress which ate raw meat during the last few years of a Democratic administration has shown that it is not going back to a milk diet just because the Republicans are in power. Nor would it do so even in wartime unless compelled, as it has been compelled by every strong President. Until the question whether it would be so compelled again may arise, we might reflect that all the periods of Congressional government in our history have been periods either of bad government or of do-nothing government. There have been times when we could afford a do-nothing government; we can afford it no longer. Still less a bad government.

But to return from this digression into the factors that will make it practically possible—or practically impossible—to save us; back to the original question, Why should we be saved? What have we got that our adversaries have not that makes us worth saving? Our faults, God knows, are numerous and glaring enough; recognition of those faults is the chief cause of the loss of confidence that has afflicted so many people of the Western world. But we do recognize them; we do not pretend that our failures were decreed by ineluctable historical necessity; nor do we rewrite history according to the precepts of Doublethink, to prove that they never happened at all.

What we have to offer, to the contemporary world and to the future, is a method—and the freedom of the mind that makes that method possible. Not an infallible method, but the best yet discovered for reaching increasingly closer approximations to the truth. It will never offer its conclusions with such assurance as does dialectical materialism—which, by a singular coincidence, always seems to produce the conclusions that are convenient for the men in power. It can only say, We have kept the door open for exploration of all possibilities, consideration of all objections, application of all possible tests; and this is what seems to be true. Maybe something else will seem more probable later on, but this is the best we can do now. Or, as the method was summarized long ago—Prove all things; hold fast that which is good.

This method has been responsible for almost all human progress. Outside the Western world it does not exist, except in those parts of the East which have been influenced by Western thought; if it died here, it would die there too. Ex-President Conant of Harvard has remarked that the right to think and question and investiga.e is the basic difference between the free world and the world of totalitarianism. It might well be the basic difference that would save us, if it came to a shooting war; and whether it does that or not, this one thing—the scientific method, and above all the freedom of the mind that makes it possible—is what makes us worth saving. As G. F. Hudson has observed, "To repudiate faith in freedom is to abandon Western civilization."

The founders of this republic held that faith so firmly that its guarantee was embedded in the very first amendment to the Constitution, almost as soon as the Constitution was adopted. Yet lately that faith has been repudiated by many of our fellow citizens, if indeed they ever held it, and in that repudiation lies our greatest danger; it is this, rather than any external attack, that might bring us down. That repudiation takes various forms and appears on various levels. One phase of it was the recent attack on the Bureau of Standards and particularly the manner in which the Secretary of Commerce questioned its objectivity. As Eugene Rabinowitch commented in the *Bulletin of the Atomic Scientists,* the government has the right, if it should so choose, to subordinate the findings of science to the demands of business; but it has no right to attempt to coerce the scientists into adjusting their findings to those demands. That is Lysenkoism; it is something we had better leave to the enemy. Happily, the Secretary of Commerce now seems to have come around to that point of view.

But far more widespread and more dangerous is the general attack on the freedom of the mind. George Kennan said at Notre Dame that it springs from forces too diffuse to be described by their association

225

with the name of any one man or any one political concept—forces which perhaps were summarized by John Duncan Miller of the London *Times,* in the early days of McCarthyism, as a revolt of the primitives against intelligence. Unfortunately, it cannot be denied that after centuries of education we will have plenty of primitives—some of them white-collar or even top-hat primitives; a sediment, a sludge, at the bottom of American society—and I am afraid a fairly deep layer at that; people who seem actuated only by hatred and fear and envy. All the products of ignorance, for their fear is not a rational fear of a very formidable and unfriendly foreign power. I have received thousands of letters from people like that in recent years and they do not seem interested in Russia at all: what they hate and fear is their own neighbors who try to think. In the name of anti-Communism they try to strike down the freedom of the mind, which above all things differentiates us from the Communists; in the name of Americanism they try to suppress the right to think what you like and say what you think, in the evident conviction—in so far as they have reasoned conviction at all—that the principles on which this Republic was founded and has been operated will not bear examination. People like that are not merely un-American; they are anti-American.

226

It is people who feel that way who provide the mass support for McCarthy—though of course he has an elite support as well, if it may be so termed, in the reactionary press and the Texas oil billionaries. He has already done serious injury to the United States Government—especially to the State Department, on which we must chiefly rely for avoidance of war; and he has done more than any other man to encourage the spread of suspicion and distrust and hatred among ourselves, which is the best formula for losing a war.

We have now reached the point where, if agents of the FBI appear in the home town of a prominent man and begin asking questions about him, his neighbors know that he is either on his way to jail or to high public office. I doubt if such confusion is healthy. Judge Learned Hand, in that speech I mentioned earlier, a speech so often quoted that perhaps everybody now knows it by heart, has said that he believes that that community is already in process of dissolution where each man begins to eye his neighbor as a possible enemy, where nonconformity with the accepted creed is a mark of disaffection, where denunciation takes the place of evidence and orthodoxy chokes freedom of dissent.

If we are not to become such a community, the friends of freedom will have to stand up and fight.

In saying all this I am talking not about Western civilization but about the United States. And without apology, for we are the principal component of Western civilization, at least in the material sense. If we go down it all goes down—and when we confront a totalitarian dictatorship, whatever goes down stays down; it doesn't get up again. And we shall go down, unless we recognize what we have to fight for and have the courage to fight for it. What makes Western civilization worth saving is the freedom of the mind, now under heavy attack from the primitives—including some university graduates—who have persisted among us. If we have not the courage to defend that faith, it won't matter much whether we are saved or not.

I do not think Stalin could have licked us; I do not think that whoever now may be running Russia can lick us. But McCarthy and the spirit of McCarthyism could lick us—no doubt without intention, but they could—by getting us to fighting among ourselves like the Romans, by persuading every man that he must keep on looking over his shoulder, to make sure that the man beside him doesn't stab him in the back. There is still enough vitality in Western civilization to save us, unless we insist on disemboweling ourselves.

I should perhaps have begun this sermon with a

text, a text taken from the fourth chapter of the first book of Samuel, the eighth and ninth verses—the mutual exhortations of the Philistines before the battle of Ebenezer. "Woe unto us!" they said when they realized that the Israelites had brought the Ark of God with them to battle. "Woe unto us! Who shall deliver us out of the hands of these mighty gods?" But then, realizing that nobody else was going to deliver them, they said to one another, "Be strong, and quit yourselves like men; and fight." And they did fight, and delivered themselves. So may we; but only if we quit ourselves like men. This republic was not established by cowards; and cowards will not preserve it.